NATIVE
AMERICAN
RELIGIOUS TRADITIONS

RELIGIONS OF THE WORLD

Series Editor: Ninian Smart
Associate Editor: Richard D. Hecht

NATIVE AMERICAN

RELIGIOUS TRADITIONS

Suzanne J. Crawford

Pacific Lutheran University, Tacoma, WA

PEARSON

Prentice
Hall

Prentice Hall Inc., Upper Saddle River, NJ 07458

Library of Congress Cataloging-in-Publication Data

Crawford, Suzanne J.
    Native American religious traditions / Suzanne Crawford.
      p. cm. -- (Religions of the world)
    Includes bibliographical references and index.
    ISBN 0–13–183483–5
    1. Indians of North America--Religion. I. Title. II. Religions of the world (Upper Saddle River, N.J.)

E98.R3C757 2006
299.7--dc22

                                                                                2005047627

Editorial Director: Charlyce Jones Owen
Editorial Assistant: Carla Worner
Marketing Assistant: Jennifer Lang

Pearson Education LTD.   Pearson Education, Canada, Ltd
Pearson Education Australia PTY, Limited   Pearson Educación de Mexico, S.A. de C.V.
Pearson Education Singapore, Pte. Ltd   Pearson Education–Japan
Pearson Education North Asia Ltd   Pearson Education Malaysia, Pte. Ltd

This book was designed and produced by
Laurence King Publishing Ltd., London
www.laurenceking.co.uk

Every effort has been made to contact the copyright holders, but should there be any errors or omissions,
Laurence King Publishing Ltd. would be pleased to insert the appropriate acknowledgment in any subsequent
printing of this publication.

Editor: Christine Davis
Commissioning Editor: Melanie White
Picture Researcher: Sue Bolsom
Designer: Andrew Shoolbred
Maps: Advanced Illustration

Reviewers: Barbara Darling-Smith, Wheaton College; James E. Huchingson, Florida International University;
Bruce E. Johansen, University of Nebraska at Omaha; Benjamin R. Kracht, Northeastern State University;
Carl Olson, Allegheny College; Pamela Jean Owens, University of Nebraska at Omaha; John Barry Ryan,
Manhattan College; Calbert A. Seciwa, Arizona State University

Picture Credits: *Cover and page 33* © Richard Cummins/CORBIS; *page 26* © Natalie Forbes/CORBIS;
page 74 LKP archives; *page 87* © Bettmann/CORBIS; *page 98* © Photograph by Karl W. Luckert, originally
published in Karl Luckert, *Coyoteway* (Tucson: University of Arizona Press, 1979); *page 108* © Susan Point;
page 114 © Jimi Lott/The Seattle Times; *page 122* © Seattle Post-Intelligencer Collection/CORBIS

Contents

4: Contemporary and Traditional: Native American Religious Traditions Today   84

5: Sovereignty, Ecology, and Religious Freedom in the Next Millennium   105

Foreword

Religions of the World

The informed citizen or student needs a good overall knowledge of our small but complicated world. Fifty years ago you might have neglected religions. Now, however, we are shrewder and can see that religions and ideologies not only form civilizations but directly influence international events. These brief books provide succinct, balanced, and informative guides to the major faiths and one volume also introduces the changing religious scene as we enter the new millennium.

Today we want not only to be informed, but to be stimulated by the life and beliefs of the diverse and often complex religions of today's world. These insightful and accessible introductions allow you to explore the riches of each tradition—to understand its history, its beliefs and practices, and also to grasp its influence upon the modern world. The books have been written by a team of excellent and, on the whole, younger scholars, who represent a new generation of writers in the field of religious studies. While aware of the political and historical influences of religion, these authors aim to present the religion's spiritual side in a fresh and interesting way. So, whether you are interested simply in descriptive knowledge of a faith, or in exploring its spiritual message, you will find these introductions invaluable.

The emphasis in these books is on the modern period, because every religious tradition has transformed itself in the face of the traumatic experiences of the last two hundred years or more. Colonialism, industrialization, nationalism, revivals of religion, new religions, world wars, revolutions, and social transformations have not left faith unaffected and have drawn on religious and anti-religious forces to reshape our world. Modern technology in the last twenty-five years—from the Boeing 747 to the world wide web—has made our globe seem a much smaller place. Even the Moon's magic has been captured by technology.

We meet in these books people of the modern period as a sample of the many changes over the last few centuries. At the same time, each book provides a valuable insight into the different dimensions of the religion: its teachings, narratives, organizations, rituals, and experiences. In touching on these features, each volume gives a rounded view of the tradition, enabling you to understand what it means to belong to a particular faith. As the Native American proverb has it: "Never judge a person without walking a mile in his moccasins."

To assist you further in your exploration, a number of useful reference aids are included. Each book contains a chronology, maps, glossary, pronunciation or transliteration guide, reading list, and index, while a selection of images provide examples of religious art, symbols, and contemporary practices.

I hope you will find these introductions enjoyable and illuminating. Brevity is supposed to be the soul of wit: it can also turn out to be what we need in the first instance in introducing cultural and spiritual themes.

Ninian Smart
Santa Barbara, 1998

Preface

This book is an introduction to the Native traditions, cultures, and histories of North America. In such a small volume it is difficult to attempt a proper discussion of such diverse populations, or fully to relate the complicated and painful history that the First Peoples of this region have endured under the colonial presence of the United States. By focusing on key themes, broad movements, and central events, this book attempts to do so. It seeks primarily to illustrate the relationship between Native peoples and the land on which they have lived for thousands of years, and the ways in which Native communities have struggled to retain their sovereignty and revive their cultural traditions. Growing up in the Pacific Northwest I was surrounded by examples of this, where local Native communities fought to keep their long-established fishing rights and then organized themselves to protect the habitats of those fish, as well as their own ceremonial systems which had helped to preserve their relationships with them. It inspired me to learn more.

But writing and publishing on Native traditions is a complicated endeavor. Many traditional community leaders have protested the publication of material that revealed too much information about sacred ceremonies, beliefs, and practices, or that represented those traditions in ways that were inaccurate, or misleading. Good scholarship on indigenous traditions recognizes this, and works closely with Native communities and elders to put forth only that information approved for sharing with a larger audience, and vetted by community elders and spiritual leaders. To do such work requires years of commitment to Native communities, and careful collaboration with indigenous cultural experts. Fortunately for those interested in increasing intercultural awareness, such scholarship by both Native and non-Native authors does exist. However, particularly given the wide array of New Age publications on the subject, the most difficult part of learning about indigenous religious life can be simply locating this good work, and separating it from publications undertaken without the participation or approval of the indigenous communities and traditions they claim to describe.

Out of respect for the religious privacy of the indigenous communities discussed in this book, and with the hope of guiding students toward examples of solid, respectful, and careful research, this book is drawn from previously published sources written by authors highly respected by both academic scholars and Native communities, exemplars of ethical scholarship done with a commitment to the well-being of Native nations. A secondary goal of this book is thus to introduce students to some reliable resources for further reading and research. I have done my best to omit any material from this book that would be seen as compromising the spiritual and cultural privacy of Native traditions, including only information that has been approved for publication elsewhere. I also recognize that writing about Native religious traditions at all, even in the general way in which I have tried to do so here, may be offensive to some. But, I continue to believe in the importance of teaching non-Native people about indigenous traditions—both to promote cross-cultural awareness, and, importantly, so that non-Natives can comprehend the critical importance of indigenous political battles currently being fought, such as the protection of sacred lands and resources, subsistence fishing and hunting rights, repatriation and reburial, and the revival of indigenous languages. As a teacher, I struggle to achieve this in the classroom as well. While my students do not need to know the intimate details of a particular ceremonial activity honoring the role of old growth cedar in Coast Salish traditions, for instance, I do want them to understand the central role of such species within Native traditions so that they can have a fuller and more profound empathy for the reasons why these species must be protected. In some small way, I hope this book contributes to that growing awareness and a broader support for Native rights.

In writing this book it has been my goal to describe the histories and spiritual traditions in ways that faithfully represent the perspective of the Native communities themselves, for they are the true experts. But readers should keep in mind that what is presented in these pages is, ultimately, a single interpretation of these traditions, viewed through the lens of my own positioning. As such it is partial and incomplete. It is not conclusive, and far from exhaustive. In my work, I seek to honor my own Native heritage (my grandfather Homer Crawford was a descendant of the Kaw Nation), but it should be noted that I am not a registered member of any Native nation, nor have I lived within a reservation community. I am thus an outsider to these traditions, but one who has done her best to approach them humbly and with great care.[1]

Special thanks are due to Raymond Bucko (Creighton University), Lee Irwin (College of Charleston), Charlotte Cote (University of Washington), Coll-Peter Thrush (University of Washington), Dennis F. Kelley (University of Missouri), Patricia O'Connell Killen (Pacific Lutheran University), Pamela Jean Owens (University of Nebraska), Nancy Parezo (University of Arizona), and Inés Talamantez (University of California, Santa Barbara), for reading drafts of chapters and offering suggestions for material in this volume. Thanks as well to Melanie White, editor at Laurence King, and to the reviewers commissioned by the press who offered invaluable advice and critique. Any remaining errors, omissions, and misstatements, are, of course, my own.

This book is dedicated to Jeanne Sylvia Crawford and Timothy Homer Crawford, for their love, support, and constant encouragement. And finally, *Do mo čara dil Mičeal Taidg Uí Briain, le lán grád mo croide, ó, Suzanne.*

Suzanne J. Crawford
February 2005

---

1   A note for educators: One of the greatest challenges in writing a book of this length was to limit my discussion to only three Native traditions. Many educators may wish to use this book as a jumping-off point, providing a structure and background with which to approach other, perhaps local, traditions.

Timeline

1608	Earliest missions to North America. French Jesuits in New France.
1680	Pueblo Revolt. Led by Popé, the Pueblo people expel the Franciscans and Spaniards from present-day New Mexico.
1800	Sganyajai:yo, Handsome Lake (1735–1815) founds the Iroquois Longhouse Religion.
1819	Indian Civilization Fund Act established by Congress to teach Native people farming and animal husbandry, and to integrate them into U.S. economy and culture.
1830	Indian Removal Bill: aims to remove Choctaws, Chickasaws, Creeks, and Seminoles west to Indian Territory.
1838	"Trail of Tears": the forcible removal of the Cherokee people to Indian Territory in present-day Oklahoma.
1850	Most Native nations assigned to reservations by this date.
1863– 1864	Kit Carson leads devastating attacks against the Diné, culminating in their forced relocation to Bosque Redondo, known as "The Long Walk." Nearly 25% of the population die during their exile.
1868	The Diné return to their traditional homeland.
1868	Surgeon General's Order directs United States army to collect human remains, particularly crania of American Indians, and return them to Washington D.C. for study.
1868	Lakota sign the Fort Laramie Treaty, establishing the Great Sioux Reservation, encompassing the entire region of South Dakota west of the Missouri River, including the Black Hills. An Unceded Territory is also established for the Lakota's undisturbed use, covering northwest Nebraska, northeast Wyoming, and southwest Montana.
1869	Beginning of Grant's so-called Peace Policy, promoting the assimilation of Native people under the direction of Christian missionaries.
1874	General George Armstrong Custer discovers gold in the Black Hills.
1875	15,000 Euroamerican gold miners at work in the Black Hills.
1876	Battle at Little Big Horn. Custer's 7th Cavalry is defeated by Lakota warriors.
1882	"Rules for Indian Courts": The practice of Native religious traditions is outlawed, with participants liable to thirty days in prison. Spiritual leaders conducting a ceremony can be imprisoned for up to six months.
1882	On the Squaxin Island reservation, John Slocum dies and visits heaven. Receives his vision for the Indian Shaker Church.

1883 Indian Religious Crimes Code imposes prison sentences and suspends rations for those caught participating in Native ceremonies.

1887 Dawes Act, also known as General Allotment Act, breaks up communal land ownership, and assigns individual allotments to Native individuals. Married men receive 160 acres; unmarried individuals could receive up to 80. Lands are held in trust by the federal government for twenty-five years.

1889 The Paiute Wovoka receives a vision and founds his religious movement, the Ghost Dance.

1890 Massacre at Wounded Knee.

1910 Indian Shaker Church is registered with the State of Washington as a formal church, protected by U.S. Constitution.

1921 Circular 1665. Bureau of Indian Affairs directs reservation agents to suppress the practice of Native religious traditions, particularly those involving traditional dances, ceremonies, and giveaways.

1924 Citizenship is finally granted to Native American people, many of whom fought in the armed services in World War I without the benefit of citizenship.

1934 John Collier's "Wheeler–Howard Act" comes into force. It restores local governance, ends mandatory removal of children to boarding schools, ends the allotment system and works to reunite checkerboard reservation lands, reorganizes the school system, and provides scholarships for Native children to attend college. It also overturns the ban on Native American religious practices, and encourages the preservation of Native cultures and traditions.

1950s Termination and relocation policies seek to terminate tribal status, and move Native people to urban centers.

1972 Formation of the Navajo Health Association.

1977 Denver Art Museum repatriates the Zuni War Gods to the Zuni nation.

1978 Formation of the Medicine Man's Association, later renamed the Dineh Spiritual and Cultural Society.

1978 American Indian Religious Freedom Act (AIRFA) is signed into law. "On and after August 11, 1978, it shall be the policy of the United States to protect and preserve for American Indians their inherent right of freedom to believe, express, and exercise the traditional religions of the American Indian, Eskimo, Aleut, and Native Hawaiians, including but not limited to access to sites, use and possession of sacred objects, and the freedom to worship through ceremonials and traditional rites." Title 42, Chapter 21, Subchapter 1, Section 1996.

1978 Indian Child Welfare Act ends mandatory boarding schooling for Native children and a federal policy promoting the adopting of Indian children into non-Native homes.

1979 Archaeological Resources Protection Act signed into law. It requires that archaeologists consult with local Native tribes when conducting a dig, particularly when human remains are involved.

1982 United Nations Economic and Social Council establishes the Working Group on Indigenous Populations.

1990 Native American Graves Protection and Repatriation Act (NAGPRA) is signed into law. The law provides for the return of Native remains and cultural patrimony held by public institutions.

1994 Amendment to AIRFA is passed, which ensures the right of Native American Church members to have access to peyote for religious purposes. It states: "Notwithstanding any other provision of law, the use, possession, or transportation of peyote by an Indian for bona fide traditional ceremonial purposes in connection with the practice of a traditional Indian religion is lawful, and shall not be prohibited by the United States or any State. No Indian shall be penalized or discriminated against on the basis of such use, possession or transportation, including, but not limited to denial of otherwise applicable benefits under public assistance programs."

1996 The Ancient One (Kennewick Man) is discovered on the banks of the Columbia River. The nearly 10,000-year-old skeleton sets off a legal battle between anthropologists who wish to study the remains and the Army Corps of Engineers, which seeks to return the remains to Native communities for reburial.

2004 Federal judge rules that the remains of Kennewick Man are not subject to NAGPRA, and they are released to anthropologists for study.

1994– United Nations' Decade of the World's Indigenous Peoples. During this
2004 decade the UN created the Permanent Forum on Indigenous Issues, which works to promote awareness of indigenous concerns and provides recommendations to the United Nations Economic and Social Council.

N

Coast Salish region
Diné (Navajo) region
Lakota region
• Native reservation or reserve

New York

Washington

Ottawa

Toronto

Chicago

Houston

Winnipeg

CANADA

Crow Creek
SOUTH
DAKOTA   Rosebud

Standing Rock
Cheyenne River   Pine Ridge
Lower Brûlé

Denver

UNITED STATES

OF AMERICA

MEXICO

Hopi

Diné (Navajo)

ARIZONA   Phoenix

Los Angeles

BRITISH
COLUMBIA

Comox
Semiahmoo
Cowichan
Lummi
Swinomish
Upper Skagit
Stillaguamish
Nooksack
Tulalip
Sauk Suiattle
Muckleshoot
Puyallup

Seechelt   Squamish

Songish

Shuswap

Lilloet

Squamish
Songish
Jamestown Klallam
Lower Elwah
Port Gamble S'klallam
Suquamish Port Madison
Skokomish
Squaxin Island
Shoalwater Bay
Chehalis

Seattle
WASHINGTON

Nisqually

Vancouver Island

Vancouver

**Coast Salish, Lakota, and
Diné (Navajo) Reservations
and Reserves**

Religion in Action: Transcendence, Thanksgiving, and Transformation | 1

This book is an introduction to Native American religious traditions, their historical context, and how they are practiced and experienced today. It does not provide a comprehensive or exhaustive examination of these traditions, for the sheer diversity of the Native peoples of North America prevents this. There are 562 tribal nations currently recognized by the United States federal government, and 245 other tribal nations that are recognized by State governments, many of whom are currently seeking federal recognition.[1] Native America thus includes over 800 unique tribal nations, most of whom have their own distinct language, their own cultural, spiritual, and philosophical traditions, and their own worldview. It is important to remember that there is no single "Native American philosophy" or "Native American religion." These traditions differ broadly depending on where you look, and to whom you speak. The creation stories, ritual traditions, worldviews, languages, and ethical systems of these cultural groups vary enormously—as much, perhaps, as the cultures of Northern Europe might differ from those of Southeast Asia. Hence, this book does not attempt to provide a thorough overview of Native traditions as they exist in all areas of the country. Rather, it looks at three distinct Native communities living in opposite corners of North America.

A central theme of this book is that many of the differences that exist between indigenous traditions can be attributed to the very landscape within which these cultures exist. These are autochthonous traditions: traditions that emerge from the earth. Indigenous cultures share an intimacy between their spiritual and cultural traditions and the natural environment in which these traditions have taken shape. Vastly varying landscapes have thus directly contributed to the formation of incredibly diverse cultures. Cultures of the

Plains are influenced by the Great Plains themselves, their landscape, open vistas, geology, flora, and fauna. Likewise, nations of the Pacific Northwest Coast have crafted cultures built from the oceans, volcanic mountains, cedar forests, and salmon runs that surround them.

In the chapters that follow, three indigenous traditions of North America are explored at length: the **Diné**, or Navajo nation, of the Four Corners region in the Southwest; the **Coast Salish** of the Pacific Northwest Coast; and the **Lakota** of the Northern Plains.[2] Obviously, choosing these three cultural groups means that many cultures have been omitted. Very little is said here about Native communities in the Northeastern or Southeastern regions of the country, for example, and students are certainly encouraged to pursue further reading in these areas. Some suggestions for reading are included at the end of the book.

It is my hope that the chapters that follow will contribute to the growing field of Native American religious studies. Until very recently, scholarship on Native traditions was written with a distinctly Euroamerican agenda, with very few attempts to understand the traditions as they were perceived and experienced by Native people themselves. Native religious traditions were explained as primitive precursors to the Christian religion of "civilized man." Further, many ethnographers who sought to study these traditions in the late nineteenth and early twentieth centuries did so under the guise of what has been called "salvage ethnography." That is, they were guided by the belief that Native people and traditions were dying out, and would soon vanish. These were considered endangered species that had to be studied, quickly, before the "genuine" traditions were lost forever. As many Native scholars have pointed out in recent years, including Vine Deloria Jr., so-called "salvage ethnographers," while certainly well intentioned, labored under a misconception as to what "real Indian religion" was about, seeking to preserve an idealistic image of pristine culture, untouched by external influences. But Native traditions and ceremonies have always been in a state of flux and change, adapting to shifts in ecology, environment, and social interaction. Tribal nations met, exchanged knowledge, and shared traditions. The assumption that Native people and traditional Native culture were vanishing from the earth relied on a view of Native culture as static, fixed, and inherently fragile.

Colonialism, missionary expeditions, and the introduction of non-native epidemic diseases did indeed devastate Native nations. Entire communities were destroyed, and much cultural knowledge was lost. However, what is amazing is the degree to which Native people have retained their traditions, modifying and reshaping them to suit contemporary needs and issues, while maintaining core values of spirituality, wellness, and sacrality. Hence, the Sun Dance has become a ceremony that many Christian Lakota integrate into their spiritual lives, finding similarities between the sacrifice of the Sun Dancer and that of Christ. The Coast Salish First Salmon ceremony stands as a clear example of the importance of traditional ritual, ceremony, and ecological ethics in a very contemporary world. And the Diné *Kinàáldá* has also changed to accommodate new challenges that young Diné women face today, such as career choices, managing families, and avoiding dangers such as alcohol, drugs, and early pregnancy. In contrast with the static view of tradition in nineteenth- and early twentieth-century ethnographies, in the last few decades much scholarship has taken on this more fluid perspective regarding what can be defined as "traditional" Native practice, allowing for the innovation and creativity that have always been a part of Native culture. Many contemporary scholars are also working in partnership with Native communities, seeking to present Native traditions and cultures as they are seen and understood by Native people themselves, and working toward research goals that are often set by the communities with whom they work.

The goal of this volume is to demonstrate that Native people and cultures are indeed alive and thriving in the twenty-first century. They face challenges, but they are doing so by drawing upon a rich cultural heritage. This first chapter introduces three ceremonial gatherings as they occur in the lives of these communities. The aim is to place the reader within the lived experience of contemporary Native traditions, to give a sense of what a particular gathering might feel, smell, and look like. These descriptions are placed within their historical, cultural, and political context in the chapters that follow. Chapter 2 addresses the philosophical foundations of Native traditions, particularly as found within stories of origin and modes of cultivating spiritual power. Chapter 3 discusses the impact of colonialism and Christian missions on these three communities, and the ways indigenous religious traditions adapted or responded to political, economic, and environmental crises. Chapter 4 discusses contemporary American Indian traditions in the late twentieth and early twenty-first centuries, placing the ceremonies described in Chapter 1 within their broader cultural and ceremonial context. The book concludes with a final chapter expanding on important issues and challenges for the survival of Native American religious traditions in the next century, including religious freedom, the preservation of sacred spaces, and the repatriation of human remains and ceremonial objects.[3] But first, a look at religion in practice.

Religion on the ground

The Lakota Sun Dance[4]

It is midsummer, and the heat rising from the field is already overwhelming. Cars, trucks, and vans have turned off the road running through the reservation and have driven over what, for the rest of the year, is pasture for tribal bison herds. The site is far from the nearest town, and there will be no electricity or running water. As you drive over the field, you notice that families have already begun erecting tents, tipis, and campers. The steady roar of a Coleman stove reminds you of lunch, and you remember that the full moon will make flashlights unnecessary tonight.

Two ceremonial tipis have been built for the dancers, one for men and another for women. Their floors are covered with sage—and the dancers will sleep there in preparation for their work tomorrow. You have come to one of the many annual Sun Dances, *wiwanyang wacipi* ("gazing at the sun"), to watch your cousin dance. The dancers are keeping a vow they made the year before. While you will not be participating, for the next four days you will be watching, offering your prayers in support of the dancers' efforts. Although you have been living in Minneapolis for the last four years, you return to the reservation every summer for a Sun Dance. It is a time when the community comes together, when extended families restore familial bonds, when everyone pitches in to support the dancers and the sacrifices they are making on behalf of their community. You park your car and begin unloading cases of food that you have brought with you. A woman elder points you in the direction of the cooking arbor, where you leave the food with the women inside. They in turn find you an axe, and for the next several hours you are chopping firewood, hauling water, and doing as you're instructed. While men will direct the Sun Dance itself, it is women who direct the social aspects of the gathering as a whole, and young men obediently do as the elder women direct.

Later, you join in with those working to build the Sun Dance arbor, a circular shade located in front of the ceremonial tipis, built of forked posts set into the ground and covered with green boughs. Before they are set in place, the posts are blessed and prayed over, and sweetgrass is burned to purify and bless the space. The arbor is open to the east. The side opposite the entrance is reserved for *wakan* (holy) people, those participating in the dance: spiritual leaders and elders, the dancers, their advisors and teachers, the young women who have cut the sacred pole, and mothers waiting to have their young infants' ears pierced. The sides of the arbor nearest to the entrance are for observers, those not *wakan*, who will offer their emotional and spiritual support for the dancers, but generally are not allowed to set foot within the dance arena itself. The arena, the circular area within the arbor, will be the focus of the following days' activities. Once the arbor is completed, you rest in its shade, a welcome respite from the midsummer sun of the Northern Plains. As you watch, a hole is dug at the center of the arena and is consecrated with buffalo fat. This is the time when the sacred pole is brought in.

Four young men had been sent out to the sacred cottonwood tree (usually chosen in advance) to "capture" it. The tree is treated like an honored enemy: it is spoken to, prayed to, sung to, and treated with respect. A prayerful apology is given to the birds that live in its branches. Then, four young virginal women each strike one blow in each of the four directions before others cut the tree down.[5] When the tree falls, the men present catch it: it must not touch the ground. Next, it is carried to the arena. When the distance is too great, as it was this year, the tree is driven to the arena, other cars along the highway stopping in respect as the tree passed by. Along the way, those carrying the tree stop four times, and at each pause ritual songs are sung. Now, you watch as the pole is carefully erected at the center of the arena. Respectfully, the tree is honored with songs, with smoke from a sacred pipe, and with prayers to the four directions. Thus the tree and the center of the arena are consecrated as holy. The lower branches of the tree have been removed, but the topmost branches remain. In these branches, the spirit of the tree remains present, and will, along with the sun, soon become the focus of the dancers' prayers. An altar is built, and a buffalo skull is placed at the base of the tree. High on the tree is a bundle of chokecherry branches. From these, effigies of a man and a male buffalo are hung, both made from buffalo hide, symbolizing fertility and success in hunting and warfare. Streamers of cotton cloth meant as offerings hang from the branches, along with tobacco ties. Participants and observers have spent hours making these prayer ties: each one contains a pinch of tobacco, prayerfully sewn up in a small cotton pouch. The colors of the cotton cloth and tobacco ties indicate prayers to the four directions, the heavens and the earth. The meaning of the colors can differ, but one arrangement of the colors is: white, honoring the north; yellow, honoring the east; red, honoring the south; black, honoring the west; green, honoring the earth; and blue, the sky.

The dance will not begin until tomorrow, but tonight there will be a feast for those who have come to attend it. You are once again put to work, tending a fire for the cooks, hauling clean water, and removing trash. There is a lot to do, and everyone pitches in. You know that through your labor and good spirit you are giving strength to the dancers who will suffer tomorrow. By evening, everyone has arrived; there are over 200 people, and an enormous feast begins. Prayers are made, and dancers share their pledges, make their oaths, making their offerings so that the community will benefit, or so that struggling individuals will be given strength and health. Songs and prayers are sung to the beat of the drum, Sun Dance songs that have been passed down through the generations for hundreds and perhaps thousands of years. All night long, singers will drum by the fire, singing ceremonial songs.

The next morning, at 4.30, you are still asleep in your tent when you hear the wake-up call. Through bleary eyes, you see that the sun has not yet risen, and you know your cousin will be getting up and going to prepare himself. A year ago he pledged to dance. He had had a dream about the difficulties that young Lakota people face, and that through his suffering in the dance, his prayers would help to make the community stronger. There was more to the dream, but he has not shared that with you. The details are between him and his advisor, whom he calls *tunkašila*, or grandfather. But his advisor is not a genetic grandfather; he is his guide, his teacher, his mentor.

When your cousin first vowed to take part in the Sun Dance, his first obligation was to find a mentor. He visited a friend of his grandfather's, a man known for his wisdom and his experience as a Sun Dancer, taking him a gift and a ceremonial pipe filled with tobacco, formally requesting that he act as his mentor. The advisor contemplated the request for several days before arriving at your cousin's home and agreeing to mentor him. That weekend, he had held a sweat to begin your cousin's preparation for the Sun Dance. Prayers were offered with the pipe, and water was poured on the heated rocks of the sweat lodge. The breath of the rocks rose into the lodge, entering their bodies, renewing their life as they sweated. The mentor instructed your cousin to seek a vision or dream. When he did indeed experience another powerful dream, he talked it over with his mentor at great length. The symbols that your cousin today paints on his body and wears in his regalia are derived from this dream. This guidance continued throughout the year, as he advised your cousin on the construction of an altar, and in daily meditation and prayer, preparing him for today. The preparation was extensive, involving every area of his life: how he ate, how he exercised, how he interacted with his parents and family, how he approached his schoolwork, and his determination to abstain from drugs, alcohol, or harmful talk or thoughts. Once someone has pledged to dance, he or she must live in the right way, with respect for family, community, and the earth. And now your cousin is going to join the other dancers in the sweat lodge, where he will purify himself for the day ahead.

Along with the other dancers and participants, both men and women, he will fast from food and water. After sweating, the dancers will gather in the *wakan* section of the lodge and pray with the sacred pipe. His body and face are painted red, the color of sacred, power-filled things. As you enter the lodge, you pass by elders sitting next to the door, offering their silent support to the dancers, their hands occasionally lifted toward the center pole in prayer. The dancers enter the lodge from the east, walking in a sunwise motion, going to their left, toward the back of the lodge. The drum and ceremonial drumsticks have been placed to the left of the lodge entrance. Drummers and singers gather there; their drumbeats and songs will guide the dancers through the daylong ceremony. A respected spiritual leader, a medicine man with knowledge, experience, and spiritual power, leads the dance.

After sunrise, the dancers enter the arena, dancing around the central pole, every movement a concentrated prayer. You watch your cousin dancing, the rising sun heating the arena, his eyes focused on the pole, meditating on his dream. He wears a long red skirt, and his chest is bare; four eagle plumes are in his hair, and there is a wreath of sage around his head; a medicine bundle hangs around his neck. These dances will continue throughout the day as the dancers, in their *wakan* state, offer their prayers and meditate on the sacred pole. Later in the day, at the appointed time, your cousin moves forward, lying down on a buffalo robe at the base of the tree. The ceremonial leader, a wise elder who has himself participated in many Sun Dances, kneels next to him. Your cousin's skin is pierced with skewers made of eagle claws and tied to leather thongs hanging from the sacred tree.

Your cousin stands and dances around the tree, leaning back so that the skewers pull at the muscles in his chest. He continues to use the eagle-bone whistle, eagle down tied to the end of the whistle flying as he blows, emitting a high-pitched call. Men dance in a central circle around the sacred tree. Around them, in a wider circle, the women dance, some with eagle feathers attached to their bodies. Other women have chosen to give flesh offerings. Small circles of skin are cut from their arms and legs, and placed in a prayer bundle that is then hung from the central tree. Some men and women simply dance, gazing toward the sun. Each participant's dance and mode of sacrifice is different, depending on their pledge, and the guidance they had received from their advisor. In the heat of midsummer, it is no small task to dance under the sun all day long, so this in itself is one form of sacrifice.

Later in the afternoon, at the appropriate time, women who have brought their babies and small children to have their ears pierced will step forward into the arena, laying their babies on a bed of sage. A spiritual elder will pierce each child's ears, and in doing so will set the child apart as a Lakota; often, children will receive a new name at this time as well. The pierced ears serve as a sign that the child will follow the Lakota way of life, honoring Lakota traditions, and working for the well-being of her or his community. At this same time, other non-dancers may step forward to make flesh offerings, contributing their prayers and sacrifice to those of the Sun Dancers.

Everyone suffering does so to fulfill a dream, a vision, or a heart-felt desire to ease the suffering of his or her people or the earth. People pray and dance for friends or family members suffering in prison, from grief, alcoholism, illness, or old age, that they may live another winter. They pray for the struggles of their communities, and for the well-being of the next generation. They pray and sacrifice so that the community will not have to suffer, so that food will be plentiful and the people healthy. They are keeping a commitment made in prayer, honoring a promise. Observers, yourself included, watch from the arbor, lifting their hands in prayer toward the central pole. You remember reading one woman's description of her experience in the Sun Dance:

> I was looking into the clouds, into the sun. Brightness filled my mind. The sun seemed to speak: "I am the Eye of Life. I am the Soul of the Eye. I am the Life Giver!" In the almost unbear-able brightness, in the clouds, I saw people. I could see those that had died. ... I could hear the spirits speaking to me through the eagle-bone whistles. I heard no sound but the shrill cry of the eagle bones. I felt nothing and, at the same time, everything. It was then that I, a white-educated half-blood, became wholly Indian. I experienced a great rush of happiness.[6]

After dancing for some time, moving toward the pole and away from it, your cousin runs back and forth four times, the last time throwing himself back hard against the piercings, until they tear free from his skin. He continues to dance until some time later, when a break is called and he returns to the arbor, where his mentor and attendant care for him. They treat his wounds, pray with him, and speak to him for hours. The dance continues until sunset, when the dancers continue to fast, but observers will go back to their camps, make dinner, and enjoy each other's company, joking and singing until late into the night.

The dance continues for four days, with the dancers rising before dawn, to purify themselves in the sweat lodge, and continuing to fast and pray. Some will dance every day, but pierce only once; others will pierce every day. On the final day, the dancers are honored with a feast and a giveaway ceremony. Gifts are given to honor those who have given their support to the dancers: the spiritual leaders who led the ceremony, the dancers' mentors, their attendants, their families; those who have brought food, labor, and other resources to make the event possible. Dancers and their families express their respect, thanks, and faith in their community, speaking briefly about the person they would like to honor and then honoring them with gifts. The Sun Dance is an offering of pain, of suffering, of sacrifice, of labor, of time, and of material possessions, given for the well-being and sustenance of one's community and the earth.

First Salmon ceremony on Puget Sound [7]

When you got into your car this morning, it was raining—just a light drizzle. Cedar trees tower over your car, as you pull your car into the parking lot near the tribal longhouse. Drops of rainwater fall from the branches overhead, and a particularly large drop lands on the back of your neck, the cool water running under your collar, and down your back. Large ferns, rhododendron, vibrantly green moss, and bushes loaded with blackberries and huckleberries line the gravel parking lot. Your drive this morning has taken you along Puget Sound, past microbreweries and coffee roasters. Now, as you stand near the boat launch, you notice that the early morning clouds have burned off, and a brilliant blue August sky looms overhead. It's not yet noon, but already more than 200 people have arrived, and they wander around the beach and longhouse, parking their cars and getting ready to go inside. You spot the friend who invited you to the event. He comes over and shakes your hand, thanking you for coming. He and his family have spent the last two weeks fishing for salmon in the bay, hoping for a better salmon run than they've had in the recent past.

For thousands of years his people have measured the seasons by the return of the salmon. Year after year, the rivers and bays were full of salmon returning to their spawning grounds, and his Coast Salish people built an economy, a culture, and a spiritual tradition on their relationship with the fish. For a month before their arrival, all

At the culmination of the First Salmon Ceremony, Chief Salmon is carried ceremoniously into the long house, where he is greeted and honored by the assembled crowd. Honoring the first salmon caught each year continues an ancient tradition of the Coast Salish people, and assures a good relationship between the people and the salmon.

activity around the rivers was restricted—nothing polluting could be put in the water. Then, when the first salmon finally arrived, they were greeted with the **First Salmon ceremony**. Songs, prayers, and dances were performed to honor the first salmon, which was cut in a ritual manner and ceremonially celebrated, and whose remains were returned the river. But things have changed dramatically for his community since then. For nearly a century the U.S. government banned their ceremonies, and his people were forced to honor the first salmon in secret. Then, after thousands of years of abundance, the salmon fell victim to over-fishing and over-development. The rivers were dammed for hydroelectric power, and fish populations were overwhelmed by the seemingly endless demand of the non-Native market. Rivers and oceans were polluted by cities, farming, and ranching, and vital salmon habitat was lost. Today, salmon populations in the Northwest have fallen to 6% of their pre-colonial numbers.

Tribal communities, including that of your friend, voluntarily abandoned commercial salmon fishing long before the state or federal government acknowledged there was a problem. By then, it was too late for many salmon runs. Your friend works with other local tribal communities to restore salmon habitat and renew salmon runs, and he sees this First Salmon ceremony as a central part of that effort. His father and grandfather made their living catching salmon; they were able to fish nine months of the year. Today, they are lucky if they can fish for a week or two. They have been working hard to catch salmon for today's feast, but, he says as he frowns and shrugs his shoulders, there simply aren't enough anymore. They had to purchase Alaskan salmon to feed the more than 300 people that would be here today. The community has been working together throughout the year, nonetheless, to prepare for this gathering. He points to his little brother, who spent much of the last week preparing the sharpened sticks on which the salmon would be roasted. Everyone pitches in; everyone takes part.

Your friend directs you inside the longhouse, and you find a seat. The structure is enormous, open, and lined on both side with tiered benches. You sit up and toward the back, not wanting to be in the way. At noon, the ceremony begins. Nearly fifty dancers and drummers, wearing traditional button blankets, cedar hats, and masks, dance counterclockwise around two central fires, singing and shaking rattles. Their songs honor the salmon and welcome them to the community. Their red button blankets, their rhythmic dancing, and their sheer numbers set the stage for a powerful event. When the dancing has ended, a tribal leader steps forward to the center of the longhouse, between the two fires. He stands next to a circle of dancers and drummers, and addresses the crowd. He is the master of ceremonies, and he tells the story of the salmon people and the history of the ceremony.

He explains that the ceremony has existed for countless generations, to honor the return of the Chief of the Salmon People (**Haik Saib Yo Bouch**, or *Haik Ciaub Yubev*), who arrives first, as a scout for his people. If he is treated properly, his bones and skin will travel back to his village, where he will come back to life, renewed and able to return the following year. When he arrives at his undersea village, he will testify to the good care he was given. Then, his people will follow his lead and come, offering their lives to the Coast Salish people. It is a bargain that has been kept for thousands of years.

However, the bargain was put at risk when the ceremonies were banned, and the salmon were driven from the waters by overfishing and the destruction of their habitat. Individuals had practiced the ritual, quietly honoring the ceremony year after year, but the large communal gatherings had been banned by the federal government for nearly a century. It was after 1978, with the passage of the American Indian Religious Freedom Act, that Coast Salish communities officially revived the ceremony. Today, he says to the crowd, that commitment to care for the salmon is as strong as ever.

When the master of ceremonies has finished speaking, he calls all the local fishermen and women to come and stand at the center of the longhouse. Prayers are offered for their safety and well-being, and they are each blessed with a ceremonial feather that has been dipped in water. Each person stands quietly and humbly, thankful for their community's expression of support. The blessing is barely over when a young boy runs into the longhouse, nearly out of breath, and announces that the guest of honor has arrived. The Chief Salmon has come to the beach. The child leads the procession, along with a group of singers and drummers, as it moves around the longhouse and out to the beach. A ceremonial canoe is waiting in the bay, and the crowd waits as it is summoned to shore. A woman steps forward and offers a prayer to welcome the spirit of the salmon. Then, the master of ceremonies again steps forward, welcoming the salmon, the canoe, and its team of paddlers. The canoe finally arrives at shore, the Chief Salmon resting on its bow on a bed of cedar and fern.

As the salmon is carefully lifted up, a cheer comes from the crowd. The fish is carefully placed on a carved cedar platter, covered with cedar and fern fronds, and two men step forward to carry it carefully back to the longhouse. The salmon will be cut in a ritual manner,

leaving its bones and head intact, and cooked for the crow
consume. The singers and drummers then begin to sing, leading
the crowd in a song of celebration and thanksgiving. You don't know
the words, but you feel caught up in the joy of the moment. You
feel as though an honored guest has really arrived; you can imagine
the way someone might have felt long ago, welcoming this salmon
relative back to the community.

You find your friend in the crowd, and accompany him back to
the community center, where food will soon be served. You realize
you are quite hungry—the singing, dancing, and speaking have
gone on for some time, and it's long past your lunchtime. You and your
friend then wander outside to where the other salmon are cooking,
the salmon that will feed all those who have come to the gathering.
Your friend's relatives are all busy at work, tending the fires and the
thick salmon fillets that are cooking on sharpened sticks over the fire.
You look at the mounds of firewood, and feel a bit guilty that you weren't
here earlier, helping to chop it all. The ceremony makes you remember that you have an obligation to return all that you are given.
That is the message of the ceremony: that there are responsibilities
and obligations between people and the things that sustain them.
Chopping firewood would have been one small way you could have
contributed, and you promise yourself you'll be out with your friend
fishing next summer, getting ready for the ceremony. The smell of
salmon is intoxicating, and you're soon growing impatient for dinner.

Thankfully, the fish is finally ready. You go with your friend to
the community center, where the food is being laid out. As Chief
Salmon is brought into the room, he is accompanied by a group of
young children holding cedar boughs and fern fronds; they sing a
Salish welcome song for the honored guest, encouraging him to
continue to swim upstream to visit them for years to come. Before the
feast begins, everyone is offered a small bite of the Chief Salmon. You
hesitate, thinking briefly of the time your mother told you not to take
communion when you visited a Catholic church—only Catholics can
do that, she cautioned you. But the man carrying the platter encourages you: "Go ahead! Everyone is here to honor him, and this is
part of the way we do that." You take a small bite, and marvel at
the taste of the salmon, which was swimming just hours before,
now cooked the traditional way over an alderwood fire. An enormous

amount of food has been laid out: hundreds of pounds of salmon dominate the tables, as do enormous bowls full of clams and fry bread. The mood is festive; people are laughing, joking, eating. It is a far more eclectic group than you had first thought: Native people from nations as far away as the Northern Plains and the Southwest are visiting for the ceremony. There are also many people visiting from the local communities, reflecting the diverse demographics of Puget Sound.

Another tribal leader now stands to speak, welcoming everyone to the feast and encouraging them to eat. These ceremonies, he explains, were traditionally about maintaining a relationship with the salmon. But they were also about maintaining a relationship with each other. The ceremony brought people together: they had to work together to catch the fish, to prepare things for the gathering. They invited people from neighboring tribes, maybe even people they didn't get along with so well, to come and enjoy the food. They encouraged each other to remember that they all needed each other: the people need the salmon, the salmon need the people, and the people need each other. The speaker goes on to welcome people from the local communities, saying that if the salmon are to survive, if the habitat is to be brought back, we all have to work together. It will take everyone's cooperation—everyone realizing how sacred the salmon is, how important our relationship with salmon is—to bring the salmon runs back.

When the meal is over, you join the crowd and follow the drummers and singers who lead you back down to the beach, the remains of Chief Salmon carried before you on the carved cedar platter. At the water's edge, more songs and prayers are sung, honoring and thanking the Chief Salmon for his gift of his life, and asking him to send his brothers and sisters along to the people, to tell his brothers and sisters how well he was treated, and how much the Coast Salish people treasure their relationship with the salmon. You stand on the shore and watch as the remains are paddled far out into the water, where they will be returned, and *Haik Saib Yo Bouch* can begin his journey home.

The Diné *Kinàáldá*[8]

Over the past year, you have carefully packed away the hand-woven *biil*, or blanket dress, the silver and turquoise jewelry (borrowed from your mother, your sister-in-law, and your best friend), the deerskin moccasins, the sash, and the thong for your daughter's hair, setting them aside for the proper time. You have been ready for some while, so it is with little surprise that you hear the news that your daughter has come of age. She comes to you shyly, telling you the news that she has just begun her first period. There is little time to waste, and you are quickly on the phone, calling relatives, friends. This weekend, your daughter will receive her **Kinàaldá**. You call the singer who will sing over her throughout her ceremony. And you call the woman chosen to act as her mentor, her sponsor who will guide her through the ceremony and serve as her role model in life. The next day you leave for your great-aunt's home, where the *Kinàaldá* will be held, because she lives on the Diné reservation, and more importantly, because she has a **hooghan** (the traditional round, wood-frame structure used by the Diné for ceremonies).

The frenzied preparations remind you of your own *Kinàaldá*—when you were initiated into womanhood and taught the proper way to live as a Diné woman—and the sense of power and beauty you felt. You have already had long talks with your daughter about the way women's bodies are viewed and understood in Diné culture. For the Diné, women's bodies are holy, sacred, filled with power. They have the strength of creativity, of fertility. Menstruation is not dirty or shameful: it is profoundly powerful, with the ability to cure, to create, and to bring new life.

You leave in the early hours of morning, and arrive at the *hooghan* by 8 a.m. Along with the other women, you set about preparing things for the ceremony. Dozens of people will be coming tomorrow, and an enormous amount of work must be done to prepare food for them. Your mother and her sisters have gone to dig yucca root, not an easy task, and have brought it back to the *hooghan*, peeled and ready to use. At 9 a.m. the *Kinàaldá* begins. Your daughter's mentor, chosen for her strength, wisdom, good judgment, skills at weaving, and also career success (she is a tribal lawyer), will remain by your daughter's side for the next two days, making sure that she behaves appropriately, and that she understands the meaning of what she does and of what happens around her.

Your daughter is brought into the *hooghan*, and her hair is carefully brushed. Then, she is dressed in the attire that you have gathered and brought. She wears the *biil*, whose hand-woven designs represent the mountains and rain clouds hanging down to meet them. Her moccasins are of deer hide, so that she will share the qualities of the deer: she will be strong, fast, quiet, elegant, graceful, and resourceful. A sash is tied about her waist; its design represents the rainbow, and the fringe hanging from it signifies grass and flowers, all suggestive of rain and fertility. She wears silver and turquoise jewelry, so that her life will be filled with abundance. Now dressed, she kneels facing the east as her hair is brushed and tied back. Her hair is brushed in this way so that it will stay healthy, long, and thick throughout her life.

Your daughter stands while the women spread blankets on the floor of the *hooghan*, and she lies down, facing west. Because she is at the time of her menarche, your daughter's spirit and body are extremely malleable. The things that happen in the next few days, and the way in which they are done, will have an enormous impact on the kind of woman she will become. Her mentor now bends over her, massaging her body and forming her into the shape of **Changing Woman**, so that she will share in the qualities of that holy person. Changing Woman was the first to go through the *Kinààldá*, the first woman to have this ceremony. Her mentor works from her feet to her head, stretching and molding her body, so that she will be healthy, strong, able to endure, so that she will have a good voice, a good figure, so she will be lean and tall, with long hair, so that she will be a healthy mother and carry children with ease. As she massages her, she speaks prayers over your daughter: "Let her have strength." "Let her speak truthfully and with kindness." Your daughter's mentor proceeds carefully and cautiously, all of her actions done in exactly the right way, so that your daughter will grow to be a good, beautiful Diné woman.

When she has finished, your daughter stands. She is now a representative of Changing Woman, dressed as she was in the first *Kinààldá*, her body and spirit shaped into the image of Changing Woman. Young children now come forward to be stretched. In this time of her first menstruation, your daughter is filled with a sacred power to shape and heal others. Children come forward, and your daughter runs her hands up their bodies and lifts their arms in the air, stretching them so that they will grow tall and healthy. Elderly people

A Diné girl participates in a Kinàaldá. *Like many Native American traditions, this coming-of-age ceremony assures the well-being and strength of the whole community as well as the individual.*

and those who are ill come forward to be blessed, so that they can share in her creative energy, in the healing power that she embodies. You know that, in acting in this way, your daughter is learning her proper role as a Diné woman: she is one who embodies great power and ability, and she is obliged to use that strength in a generous way, to give back to her family and community. When all those wishing to be blessed have come forward, she turns to a pile of objects that people have brought to be blessed by her: shawls, blankets, watches, jewelry. Having blessed them, she returns them to their owners.

The next morning, the mentor wakes your daughter before dawn. This morning she must run from the ceremonial *hooghan* toward the east. As she runs, she is followed by a group of small children. Your daughter runs silently, with the children behind her yelling as loud as they can, trying to summon the *yeii*, the Holy People, to greet her as she runs to the east. She runs as far as she can toward the rising sun, thus assuring that she will be physically fit throughout her life, that she will have strength and endurance. When she returns to the *hooghan*, the children behind her shrieking and laughing, she is breathing heavily; her face is full of good color, and she is smiling.

Throughout the day, as she had yesterday, she will work to roast and grind corn for the *Kinààldá* cake, the cake that will bake in the earth throughout the final night of the *Kinààldá*, while she has her all-night ceremony. An enormous amount of cornmeal is needed, for the cake will be 36 inches in diameter, and nearly 5 inches thick. It will feed all of the friends and relatives who will come to support her in her ceremony. And there are many, because the power of the ceremony is increased by the number of relatives who attend. She works hard throughout the days, roasting and grinding corn until she has an enormous pile of cornmeal.

This afternoon you help your daughter mix the batter for the corn cake. It is an arduous task, and one that everyone works together to accomplish. Your son, your husband, and your nephews have been working throughout the night, cutting wood, hauling water, and tending fires. Yesterday they dug the pit for the cake, and have had a fire burning in it for over twenty-four hours, hardening and heating the earth. Now, they are busy boiling buckets of water. Your daughter distributes cornmeal to women seated in the four directions of the *hooghan*, and boiling water is poured over the meal. Women work hard to blend the batter, breaking up any lumps with their hands and speaking of good things. All the women involved in this work have agreed to speak and think only good things. Their thoughts, actions, and words will directly affect the success of the cake. Only strong, healthy, and moral women have been invited to help in this important process. Likewise, those men digging the pit, tending the fires, and boiling the water must do so with a good spirit and care. Everyone's energy will go into that cake, and its success depends on everyone working together in harmony, with good thoughts and with kindness. And the success of the cake will have great meaning for your daughter's life. If the cake is a success, then your daughter's life will be likewise. The actions, thoughts, and spirits of the entire family and community have a direct impact on her well-being. You concentrate on thinking and wishing good things for your daughter, and on doing your very best to mix the batter well.

When the batter is ready, your daughter and her sponsor cover the bottom of the pit with a clockwise spiral of corn husks. The batter is carefully poured into the pit, covering the husks. Then, your daughter blesses the cake with corn pollen, making a line from east to west, then from south to north, and finally a clockwise circle around the batter, leaving an opening to the east. She then covers the batter with another clockwise spiral of corn husks. These are covered with newspaper, which is then covered with clean soil, and finally a layer of hot ashes and coals. Your brother and son will keep a fire burning over the cake all night long. The fire must burn evenly, and at just the right temperature to cook the cake properly. They know the job is important, and they take their task very seriously.

Around 5 p.m. other family members, friends, and elders in the community begin to arrive. They are fed a meal of mutton stew, fry bread, and coffee. Gradually, more and more people arrive, until around 10.30, when the all-night ceremony begins.

Everyone enters the *hooghan*, except for those tending the fire outside. Women are seated to the north, men to the south. The ceremonial practitioner, or singer, blesses the *hooghan* with pollen in each of the four directions. Your daughter stands and walks in a clockwise motion around the *hooghan*, until she comes to sit to the left of the singer. She sits with her legs extended straight in front of her, her feet pointing up, her back straight, her hands resting palms upward on her legs. The singer blesses your daughter with corn pollen, touching the pollen to the bottom of her right foot, then left; to her right knee, then left; to her right palm, then left; to the front of her chest, to her back; to her right and left shoulders. He places a pinch of pollen in her mouth, then another on the top of her head. He sprinkles pollen to the east, offering a prayer for her strength and well-being. The pollen pouch is then passed in a clockwise motion around the *hooghan*. Everyone present takes the pouch, offers a prayer, and touches the pollen to their tongue and the top of their head, and then sprinkles a pinch in front of them.

At this time, the singer is ready to begin the songs, twenty-one in all. When he is finished singing each song, sung without error or hesitation, he repeats his pollen blessing, and passes the pollen pouch around the *hooghan*, so that all may pray and participate in the blessing. Your daughter sits quietly as he sings and prays, still holding her back straight, her palms upward, and her feet extended in front of her. When he has finished, she is asked to stand, and she steps out into the night, where she takes four deep breaths, turns slowly around in a clockwise motion, and then returns to the *hooghan*. Songs and prayers continue until dawn. You try hard to stay as long as you can, sitting like your daughter, with your legs stretched out in front of you, joining in the songs, and praying for your daughter's well-being. Periodically throughout the night people stand and leave the *hooghan* briefly to stretch, walk around in the moonlight, or drink coffee. You join them twice, stretching your tired back. But you work hard to stay in the *hooghan* throughout the night, giving your daughter all your prayers and strength.

At dawn, your daughter is roused from the meditative state that a night of singing and prayers can bring, and instructed to face the east once again while her sponsor washes her hair and her jewelry. As she is washed, the singer sings the dawn songs, welcoming the sun. Her sponsor blesses her with the yucca suds, much as the singer blessed her with pollen the night before. Then, with her hair still wet, she runs toward the east. She runs as hard and long as she is able, and as she runs, the singer sends her with the Running Song, the same song that was sung when Changing Woman ran toward the east on the morning of her *Kinaaldá*. When she has run as far as she can, your daughter stops and blesses the earth. She blesses herself with damp earth, touching her feet, her shins, her knees, her chest, her shoulders, the palms of her hands, and the top of her head. When she returns, she circles the cake in a clockwise manner and comes to stop beside her sponsor.

The singer then instructs her on how to greet the dawn with a pollen blessing: she is to hold the pollen and lift it toward the sun, while she takes four deep breaths, one for each of the four directions. Then, she is to place the pollen in her mouth, on the top of her head, and finally sprinkle a pinch of the pollen on the earth. When she has done this, everyone present has an opportunity to do the same. In this gesture, everyone honors and gives thanks to the corn, to its fertility, to the earth and its creative power, to the four directions and all the holy people that live in the mountains that border the Diné landscape.

The cake is now ready, and your daughter and her sponsor cut it. They sprinkle a bit of the cake on the earth, thanking it for providing them with food and life. Your daughter then distributes pieces to everyone in attendance, thanking them for their presence, their prayers and the energy that they have brought to her *Kináaldá*. The singer is given the central piece. Your daughter will not eat any of her cake herself: it is a lesson in generosity, in giving, in providing for her family and her community, and in putting their needs before her own.

When the cake has been consumed, your daughter is once again brought into the *hooghan*, and her sponsor once more brushes and combs her hair. Her face and body are painted with colors. Those in attendance come forward to be painted as well, and your daughter paints the same natural pigments across their cheeks. She is again directed to lie down on blankets facing the west, and her sponsor massages her body one last time, again shaping her into the image of Changing Woman. She molds her body, imparting to her a strong, healthy life, a tall lean physique, good words, good thoughts, and strong character. She must take this shaping with her, growing to fill these responsibilities and blessings throughout her life. Once again empowered with the presence of Changing Woman, she stretches children, drawing her hands up their bodies so that they will grow to be strong and healthy. And she blesses the elderly and ill, imparting her rejuvenating power. She again blesses and returns the objects that people have brought: blankets, shawls, jewelry, watches, wallets. Again she kneels, and her hair is brushed a final time, before being carefully retied at the back of her neck.

Following the ceremony, you will spend the next four days with your daughter and her sponsor in quiet solitude. Your daughter will take the time to reflect on the *Kinaaldá*, on its meaning, on the woman she is to become.

Conclusion

The following four chapters explain more about the ceremonies described here, and the cultures within which they occur. They examine the creation stories, oral traditions, sacred geographies, rituals, and ceremonies that form the religious milieu of the Lakota, Coast Salish, and Diné. These traditions emerge from cultures hundreds of miles apart from each other. Each culture has its own language, history, and worldview. The ceremonies described are very different in their approach, their expression, their symbols, and their meaning. Yet certain similarities can be seen within these traditions, characteristics shared by many Native American traditions. For instance, these ceremonies focus on individual well-being, but always with a wider vision toward community well-being. The sacrifices of the Sun Dance, the thanksgiving offered at the First Salmon ceremony, the importance of a young woman being shaped in the image of Changing Woman, all have as their ultimate concern a healthy community. Individuals always seek their own spiritual health and empowerment so that they may give back to their communities and families. And in these instances, "community" is not a narrowly defined human community but one that encompasses relationships with the spiritual world and with the ecological landscape.

Secondly, these ceremonial traditions are not easy. They are challenging, difficult, at times even painful. They demand an enormous amount of physical stamina, of familial support, of financial and temporal resources. They all require an extensive network of friends and family who are willing and able to take days or weeks out of their busy lives to offer support and help. They require the knowledge and assistance of spiritual elders, who guide younger people through these ceremonies and offer wisdom for them as they live their lives. No one attempts spirituality alone or in isolation. Even the solitary vision quest occurs with the guidance and support of spiritual elders. Food, feasting, and giveaways are a clear part of these events, and those who plan them give generously to everyone who participates and offers their emotional and spiritual support. As such, these are ceremonies that should never be undertaken without the guidance and direction of Native elders and community members: they are meant to be practiced only within the cultural communities from which they come.

Thirdly, these ceremonies also all rely on the reality and material presence of spiritual beings. The presence of the ancestors, the spirit of the cottonwood tree, and the buffalo are literally present with those dancing the Sun Dance; the spirit of King Salmon is literally present at the honoring ceremony; and the Holy People are welcomed to the *Kinààldá*. These are not metaphorical or symbolic gestures, but experiences built on the real presence of powerful spiritual entities.

And finally, all of these ceremonies demonstrate the autochthonous nature of these religious and cultural traditions. They emerge from the land and resources upon which the people depend for life: the open plains, the bison, the oceans, rivers, and watersheds that sustain salmon, and the corn and sheep that form such an important part of the traditional Diné economy and culture. All of these elements—community well-being, diligence, and struggle; the guidance of elders; the presence of powerful spiritual entities; and the reliance on and interdependence with the land—will be key themes in the chapters to come.

Philosophical Foundations: Religion as Relationship   2

Before the arrival of Europeans in North America, the indigenous people of this continent lived for thousands of years, developing complex social and cultural systems that enabled them to survive in a meaningful way in their native landscapes. Over time Native communities moved and migrated throughout the continent, forming alliances and creating new tribal nations. Their experiences were distinctly shaped by the places in which they lived, as they formed

symbiotic relationships with the landscape and drew their religious experiences, symbols, and stories from their surrounding environment. Because of the autochthonous relationship between Native cultures and their landscapes, Native religious traditions came to vary as widely as the landscapes of North America.

This chapter looks at some of the foundational principles of three Native spiritual and cultural traditions: the Lakota, the Diné, and the Coast Salish.[1] In order to explain the foundational worldviews that inform these religious traditions, it begins by looking at the creation narratives that describe both the origins of the people and their relationship to their landbase. It then examines the fundamental principle of sacrality or power as it exists within these traditions, and the ways in which Native people connect to and maintain a connection with this power. Power in Native religious traditions is not social or political, involving control over other people. Rather, it is an abstract energy, a force that is given and derived from the spiritual realm, a force that may be channeled through a human being. Power is temporary, earned, and lasts only so long as one maintains a relationship of respectful reciprocity with it or its source. In many Native cultures, it is the animating force of the universe, the spiritual principle that unites all things. But understanding spiritual power, where it comes from, and how it is to be approached, first requires an understanding of origins—of where these communities and their worldviews have come from.

Lakota origins²

According to one well-known version of the Lakota origin story, at first there was *Iyan* (Rock).³ *Iyan* opened itself up, and bled blue and green, creating *Mahpiyato* (Sky) and *Maka Ina* (Mother Earth). The earth and sky were formed but were lifeless, without motion. *Iyan* opened itself again, and out flowed *taku skan skan*, the spirit of *Iyan*. This spirit entered *Mahpiyato* and *Maka Ina*, giving breath and spirit to every stone, every plant, every animal: every thing in the earth and sky became a living thing. *Mahpiyato* and *Maka Ina* came together and created *Taté* (Wind), *Anpetu Wi* (Sun), *Hanhepi Wi* (Moon), and *Pté Oyaté*, the Buffalo Nation, the first people. They created *Wazi* (Old Man) and *Wakanka* (Old Woman), the first of the Buffalo Nation. These were the first people, and they were siblings to Sun, Moon, and Wind. *Wazi* and *Wakanka* had a child, *Ité*, a beautiful young woman. *Ité* married *Taté*, and they had five children: East Wind, South Wind, North Wind, West Wind, and Whirlwind.

All was well for some time, until **Iktomi** (Spider), the trickster, convinced *Wakanka* that her daughter should have married *Anpetu Wi,* the sun. Sun, *Iktomi* whispered in her ear, is far more beautiful, more majestic. *Iktomi* schemed and through his magic convinced Sun to fall in love with *Ité*. When *Ité* took Moon's seat next to Sun at a feast, breaking important rules of kinship and decorum, Moon was bitterly shamefaced and angry, refusing to come near the Sun again. Still today, when he comes close, she disappears altogether. The careful social balance that had existed in the early days of creation was threatened until *Mahpiyato* intervened, punishing everyone involved. Sun and Moon would be separated, Father Sky decreed, never to see each other again. Though Sun would relentlessly pursue Moon for eons to come, he would never overtake her. Old Man, Old Woman, and *Ité*, whose presence nearly caused cosmological chaos, were banished to wander the corners of the earth.

These First People were sent from their underworld home, leaving the rest of the Buffalo Nation behind, and found themselves on the earth's surface. *Mahpiyato* decreed that *Wazi*, *Wakanka*, and *Ité* must live as nomadic people, constantly moving from place to place throughout the great Northern Plains. To soothe his injured pride, *Taté* was given custody of his five children, the winds, and they were sent to earth as well, to do their father's bidding. For her lack of fidelity *Ité* was given a new name, *Anog-Ité*, or Double Face, and her physical appearance dramatically changed: from then on she would appear beautiful and young on one side of her face, and withered and ugly on the other.

Anog-Ité wandered the earth, but after a time she became lonely. Longing for other human company, she conspired with *Iktomi* to lure the rest of the Buffalo Nation to the earth's surface. Although the land was barren and food was rare, *Iktomi* butchered and roasted a buffalo, then made a beautiful robe out of its hide. The smell of the cooking meat wafted to the underworld, where the Buffalo People lived in comfort and peace. *Tokahé*, First Man, the Chief of the Buffalo Nation, smelled the meat and followed its scent to the surface. Having seen the food and the beautiful hide, he took them and brought them back to the Buffalo Nation. His wife and six other couples marveled at the meat and the robe, having never seen anything like it. The surface world must be an amazing place, they thought, filled with such abundance. Convinced that it was right to leave their home behind and journey to the surface, the seven couples said goodbye to the rest of the Buffalo Nation and journeyed to the surface. When they arrived, they were bitterly surprised. They found themselves in the midst of a Northern Plains winter, and were utterly unprepared for the cold, the sharp winds, and the lack of food. Desperately they tried to find their way back to the spirit world, but they were lost. Old Man and Old Woman were aware of their situation however, and came to find their children. They taught them how to survive in the harsh landscape of the Northern Plains, migrating with the changing of the seasons, and returning periodically to the Black Hills, the place where they emerged from the underworld, for ceremonies and spiritual journeys. These seven couples went on to found the seven sacred fires, the *Oceti Sakowin*, of the Buffalo Nation: *Mnicoujou* (Plants by the Water), *O'Ohenumpa* (Two Kettle), *Itazipco* (No Bows), *Sihasapa* (Blackfoot), *Oglala* (Scatters Their Own), *Sicangu* (Burnt Thighs), and *Hunkpapa* (Camps at the Entrance).

Descendants of the Buffalo Nation survived, and for hundreds of years the Buffalo Nation migrated throughout the Plains and Northern Woodlands. However, food was scarce, and the people suffered greatly. One winter, the people were very hungry and desperate for help. They sent two men out in search of food. As they walked across the Plains, the men saw someone approaching. As they drew nearer, they realized it was a beautiful woman. According to some versions of the story, one of the men, with evil in his heart, determined to have his way with her. His companion tried to deter him, but the man was insistent. When this ill-intentioned man approached the woman, a mist descended from the sky, covering both of them. When it lifted, the woman was standing, but the man had been reduced to a pile of bones. The second man fell to his knees, aware now that this was a holy woman. She directed him to return to his people and tell them that she would arrive soon, and that they should prepare themselves.

The woman was **White Buffalo Calf Woman**. When she arrived at their village, the people, although they had very little food and water, gave her all they had. In return, White Buffalo Calf Woman gave a sacred pipe to the people and instructed them how they were to pray with it. She taught them seven sacred ceremonies that they were to practice, ceremonies that would bring them well-being and comfort in life. Finally, she left the village, walking toward the Plains. As the people watched, she dropped to the ground and rolled toward the north, becoming a white buffalo. Then she rolled to the east, becoming a yellow buffalo; to the south, becoming a red buffalo; and finally to the west, becoming a black buffalo. She instructed the people in the way of hunting the buffalo, and taught them to do so with care and respect, because they themselves were descendants of the Buffalo Nation.

Sacred power on the Northern Plains

This version of the creation story of the Lakota provides a necessary foundation for understanding traditional religious practices among the Lakota people. The key elements of the story help to illuminate foundational philosophical principles of Lakota tradition. From the creative opening of *Iyan* came the cosmos. Everything within the cosmos is thus related, and animated by the spiritual energy of *Iyan*. Hence, the Lakota today often refer to "all my relations" ("**Mitakuye Oyasin**") in their prayers, recognizing this interrelatedness of all things. The fundamental energy released by *Iyan* is found throughout the cosmos, taking a unique form and expression within every spiritual and material entity: minerals, plants, animals, and forces of nature. Accessing, cultivating, and maintaining reciprocity with the sources of such power are the focus of Lakota practice. A sense of this invisible energy or life-force is often expressed in the Lakota term *wakan*. When thought of as a unified whole, in its original and ultimately unified form, this sacred power is referred to as **Wakan Tanka**, which is sometimes roughly translated as "the sum of all things unknown."

Wakan refers both to the abstract powerful energy that permeates all things in the universe and to a state of being. If objects or individuals are imbued with this power, they are referred to as *wakan*. This word has been translated by Christian scholars as "holy," but that translation draws heavily on the Western Christian tradition. In Lakota parlance, *wakan* refers to a state of empowerment with the creative life-force or energy from which the universe is created and by which it continues to be animated and held in place. This power both animates the universe, giving all things motion and breath, and also shapes it, maintaining cosmological order and placing creatures, natural forces, and elements of the landscape in their proper place.[4] Hence, Lakota traditions revere forces and objects of nature, such as Sun, Wind, and Thunder, but these traditions also refer to a broader sense of power that permeates the universe, less easy to define but nonetheless very real.

The ceremonies given by White Buffalo Calf Woman, which have been practiced by the Lakota for hundreds, perhaps thousands, of years, are a means of achieving and maintaining a state of **wolakota**, balance or harmony. The contemporary practice of the sacred ceremonies that were brought by White Buffalo Calf Woman is discussed in more detail below, in Chapter 4. For now, it is important to understand how two of these ceremonies relate to the foundations of Lakota spirituality, the creation narrative and the principles of sacred power, *wakan*.[5]

To renew one's life: *Inipi*

The practice and meaning of the sweat lodge is intricately tied to the Lakota creation story. Every time an *Inipi* or *Inikagapi* (literally, "to make or renew life force") is performed, the sacred story of creation is revisited. A round lodge is built from bent poles and covered with boughs, hides, or blankets. Stones are heated in a sacred pit, then placed within the lodge in a ceremonial manner. Participants enter the lodge naked and sit in the darkness under the round dome of the lodge, with rock, *Iyan*, at the center, just as it was at the moment of creation. Water is poured on the heated rocks, releasing the breath of *Iyan* in the form of steam. Moving in a clockwise manner, everyone present offers prayers and songs, voicing their concerns for their people. Four such prayer rounds are offered, as the participants breathe in the spirit of the stones. Ritually reenacting this moment of creation gives the prayers special efficacy, and the breath of the rocks cleanses those present, both internally and externally. Often, at the third round of the ceremony, a sacred pipe is brought into the lodge, and prayers are offered with tobacco and smoke, which carries the prayers to the spirit world.

Crying for a dream: *Hanbleceyapi*

An important theme of Lakota spirituality is that of suffering. Enduring and expressing anguish are sacred activities. Heartfelt suffering of the individual within ceremony and prayer works to mediate the suffering of the wider community, while drawing the attention of supernatural beings or spirits of the ancestors. The Sun Dance described in Chapter 1 is a powerful example of this. *Hanbleceyapi* (literally, "crying for a vision"), the vision quest, is another. It begins with an *Inipi*. First, an individual desiring to undertake a vision quest consults with a spiritual elder. This mentor guides him through the process of preparation. The mentor leads the individual through two rounds of the *Inipi*, praying with him in preparation for the time of fasting and isolation. The individual is then taken to a secluded spot, where he will undertake the vision quest. A buffalo skull altar may be placed in the western corner of the space. Four chokecherry or plum sticks painted red are placed in the four directions, each with sacred objects or flags tied to them, designating the space as *wakan*. In a hole at the center, the supplicant might place another chokecherry staff along with sacred tobacco. The supplicant fasts and prays in this small space for one to four days, offering a pipe to the four directions with prayers of tobacco and smoke. As the name of the ceremony suggests, supplicants literally cry for a dream, weeping and suffering in prayer and hunger, asking the spirits and ancestors for a vision, singing songs, while moving slowly between each of the four directions. When the agreed duration of the prayer-fast has passed, the individual's mentor returns to the place and leads him back to the sweat lodge, where two further rounds of the *Inipi* are performed. During this time, the supplicant shares whatever visions, dreams, or thoughts he had with a circle of wise elders, who interpret the experience and offer advice.

Just as ritual activities and the sacred spaces associated with them are concentrated locations of sacred power, so are sacred bundles and pipes. Although sacred bundles are relatively rare among the Lakota (with the exception of those bundles dedicated to White Buffalo Calf Woman), they serve as important foci of ritual activity for many Northern Plains people, who see them as material manifestations of sacred power. Guided by dreams and visions, an individual may compile a sacred bundle containing symbolic objects representing images from a vision: minerals, plants, or parts of an animal. Songs may also be received during prayers and visions, songs that accompany the opening or displaying of the objects in the bundle. Bundled objects are powerful symbols, but they are not merely symbols; they are the actual manifestation of that power in concentrated form. Furthermore, sacred pipes enable the people to pray powerfully and effectively. Prayers offered with the pipe, with tobacco and smoke, are filled with sacred power. The most important of these pipes is that given to the people by White Buffalo Calf Woman, a pipe still held and honored by the people today.

Much traditional Lakota religious life centers on cultivating personal contact with this power of *wakan* as it is manifested in various aspects of the cosmos, and on bringing that power into play in attaining a healthy life and secure community. White Buffalo Calf Woman provided a means for doing so, bringing the pipe, seven sacred ceremonies, and the buffalo to the people. Honoring one's relatives, being faithful to kinship bonds, affirming a relationship with the cosmos, and cultivating relationships with the powerful forces that fill it, assure personal and communal health.[6]

For the Lakota, the buffalo play a central role within this cosmology. The buffalo are considered relatives of the Lakota, trusted friends, and a source of life and well-being. From the buffalo came food, shelter, clothing, all the necessary elements for a life well lived. Because of this, hunting, killing, butchering, and using the buffalo in a respectful and ceremonial manner was and is a central part of Plains spirituality. Having recognized that the universe is entirely comprised of one's relatives, spirituality entails living all of one's life in a proper way, so as to maintain healthy, balanced relationships with all these spiritual entities, the state of being referred to as *wolakota*.

Coast Salish traditions[7]

The role of Transformer

According to some Coast Salish oral traditions, the first forms of life, the plant tribes, were given life by vital elements of earth, water, and air. The plant people were followed by animal people, and finally by the human people. In the mythic time before human people arrived on the scene, a central figure, known as **Transformer** or Changer, had the important task of ordering the world, giving each plant and animal the role that they were to play. In this mythic time, the world was chaotic, food was in short supply, tasks needed doing, and the people's skills were undifferentiated. Transformer gave order and form to the mythic social world, assigning appropriate tasks to the plant and animal tribes, and "oriented each life force to how its knowledge was going to help human beings survive."[8] The plant and animal people were gifted by the Great Spirit or Creator with ceremonial knowledge and the ability to obtain songs of power, and were instructed by Transformer to share this spiritual knowledge with the human people who would soon follow, and who would sorely need their help. The human people were instructed, in turn, to respect all forms of life, and care for the landscape that sustained them.

Transformer did not make the world but remade it, assigning names and form to the world's creatures: mosquito people, grizzly people, otter people, killer whale people, and so on. Changer determined the social and political structure of the cosmos, and explained how the universe was to be ordered. Many stories of origin on the Northwest Coast also point back to **Raven**, who first placed the sun in the sky, the moon in its orbit, and determined the proper path for salmon to travel. Changer established the world, preparing it for the arrival of human people and enabling their survival. Changer set up the social and spiritual laws that would govern the relationships between human people, animal people, plant people, and the spiritual beings of the natural world such as thunder, mountains, or lakes

It was in this mythic time, when Changer was establishing the social order of the cosmos, that the first human people negotiated their relationships with various animal people. During this time the separation between them was less great: people could speak the same language as animals, visited the villages of the animal people on a relatively frequent basis, and occasionally intermarried with them. These ancestors brought back crests, power emblems, sacred songs, dances, and masks from their animal-people relatives, and with them special spirit powers that gave them success in life. These animal people, while seen less often in the post-mythical era, are still spiritually present within the animals and plants that Coast Salish people depend on for their subsistence, such as salmon, cedar, halibut, sturgeon, and deer. As long as these relationships are honored, the Coast Salish people can procure the goodwill and powerful assistance of animal relatives in the daily tasks of life

In Coast Salish tradition, human beings are their selves generally considered to be weak, inadequately equipped, and in need of the spiritual assistance of the animals that they seek for their sustenance. To secure the good will of the creatures that a hunter or fisherman may pursue requires behavior and ritual care in catching the animal, preparing and disposing of the remains. Traditional stories of origin instruct Salish people to approach animals with respect as animal people, and a complex series of ritual behavior governs interaction with any plant, animal, or fish that is fished or hunt. Gatherers and hunters always spoke reverently and respectfully to their game, preparing themselves ritually to capture anything.

Inhabiting the Northwest Coast, Coast Salish traditionally lived amid great abundance. The ocean of fish, seal, and shellfish, while the cedar forests bordering the shore were filled with grouse, deer, elk, and bear. This meant that, unlike the Lakota, the Coast Salish did not need to migrate. They lived in permanent villages along the coast, in large cedar-plank homes elaborately decorated with carvings and paintings that indicated the people's relationship with various animal-spirit powers. A pre-colonial home could comfortably house a village chief, his wife, their children, their children's spouses, and their grandchildren, as well as several slaves. In many Northwest Coastal cultures, homes and property were jointly owned by a husband and his wife, though inheritance and clan affiliation were usually passed through the woman's lineage. Children took their mother's name and would inherit their rank and wealth from their maternal uncle. Traditional Coast Salish society comprised a complex social hierarchy that was intricately tied to spiritual success. To attain spiritual power through good relationships with animal spirits and other spirit powers, is to gain important skills such as hunting, fishing, basketry, carving, midwifery, or wealth-acquiring. Despite the relative security and stability of Coast Salish life, the people are aware that they are utterly dependent on the animal and plant resources around them. Should the fish or animals decide not to offer themselves to the people, the people will starve. Of all the animals in this ecosystem, few hold such an important place on the Coast Salish dinner table and in their cosmology as the salmon.

Salmon spawn twice a year, swimming upriver to lay their eggs in the shoals where they themselves had previously hatched. During these times, the Coast Salish people visit traditional fishing locations, where they procure enormous amounts of fish. Salmon will be cut, dried, smoked, and stored for the winter months. However, in order for salmon to be reborn and return the following year the fish must be killed and cut in a certain manner, and then disposed of in the proper way. If treated properly, the salmon return to their undersea home, put on new flesh, and live again. The Coast Salish people thus have a reciprocal relationship with the salmon. Of course, in the contemporary era this sacred balance has been severely challenged by other threats to the survival of the salmon: unchecked population growth, over-consumption, destruction of salmon habitat, dams, and over-fishing by non-Natives.

Guardian spirits and spiritual power

For traditional Coast Salish people, survival depends on acquiring the spirit power of animals such as the salmon.[9] This can occur through inheritance from an ancestor who historically established a relationship with the animal people, or through one's own experiential interaction with powerful spirit powers. Spiritual power is embodied in the spiritual gifts and abilities that certain living beings carry and which can be given to human people. Power is an expression of relationship between an individual and a spiritual being, a testimony to the well-being of that relationship, and a mark of potential transformation. In Coast Salish traditions, power coalesces in other-than-human beings. These include beings that live under the sea, on land, and in the air, both natural beings such as killer whale and grouse, and mythical beings such as the Thunderbird. Throughout many Pacific Northwest Coastal cultures, some material objects also act as *loci* of power, such as copper, which enables the accumulation of wealth, or raven rattles (rattles in the shape of a raven), which are used by spiritual specialists. Images such as crests found on house posts, memorial poles, or house fronts can also contain power, in so far as they commemorate a relationship between an ancestor and a spirit power. When something acts as such a *locus* of concentrated power it is what Pamela Amoss has described as *xœ'xœ*: powerful, dangerous, sacred.[10] As such, it is neither inherently good nor inherently evil, but can be directed in ways that are either creative or destructive, and thus must be approached with caution and respect. For the Coast Salish, three important ceremonial modes of cultivating such power were the vision quest, winter ceremonials, and First Salmon ceremonies.

Quests for guardian spirits are an important part of traditional Coast Salish life.[11] After being carefully prepared by spiritual leaders and elders, individuals are sent to isolated places such as mountain lakes or waterfalls for several days of fasting and prayerful contemplation.[12] During this time they may tend a large fire, pray, bathe regularly, and refrain from eating or sleeping. During these vision quests, some young people receive a visionary experience of their guardian spirit power and are given a spirit power song. While one may encounter and accrue spirit powers throughout one's life, the most common times to do so are during puberty and pregnancy. During such liminal (or transformative) times, one is particularly susceptible to powerful beings, and more keenly aware of their presence. Spirit songs, crests, other dream objects, or spirit dances may also be received at this time. Seeking a guardian spirit makes sense within a philosophical framework in which all inhabitants of the earth were originally people speaking the same language and obeying the same cultural rules. Through suffering and determination, an individual can re-establish these ancestral relationships.[13] While vision quests are relatively rare in the contemporary era, Coast Salish people continue to seek spiritual power in prayer, in dreams, and by participating in winter ceremonies.

Traditionally, on returning from such a guardian spirit quest, individuals will confer with their spiritual elders, who will help them to interpret their experience. If an individual receives a spirit power, he or she may have the image of that spirit power carved onto crests, house posts, or masks. If the young person comes from a family of means, their parents may hold a **potlatch** in their honor. Potlatches are large ceremonial giveaways, designed to confer social and spiritual prestige on the giver. Through such a giveaway, the new spiritual and social positions are established and publicly acknowledged. The potlatch is an important mode in which power is given, validated, and expressed, community ties are strengthened, and spiritual relationships are affirmed.[14]

However, as many scholars have pointed out, maintaining a relationship with guardian spirits' power takes work. Such spirits must be honored and respected for the rest of one's life. In traditional Coast Salish practice, the individual periodically honors their spirit power through song and dance. Such activities frequently take place in winter ceremonials, which Pamela Amoss and Crisca Bierwert translate as **syó'wən**, a Nooksack Salish term that refers to both winter ceremonials and one's guardian spirit.[15] Winter on the Northwest Coast is a wet, cool time of year, and the days are short. Coast Salish people hold most of their ceremonial activities during the wintertime, a period when few people are occupied with hunting or fishing, and when most of the village are gathered in one place. During the summer months, many people are off in temporary fishing camps, hunting, or gathering berries and basketry materials. But winter is a perfect time to gather together, to tell stories, and to celebrate the community's guardian spirits. During these winter ceremonials, the participants eat special foods and perform the songs and dances inspired by their spirit powers.

According to narratives recorded by Pamela Amoss and Crisca Bierwert, participation in these spiritual activities is important, because spirit powers may actually cause spirit sickness if they are not allowed to express themselves through an individual in song and masked dance. Individuals are inspired or possessed by their spirit powers and celebrate their relationship with these beings in dance. First-time dancers are guided through their first syó'wən by spiritual leaders during the winter following their first vision. Winter ceremonials are vital parts of other Northwest Coast communities as well. Franz Boas recorded one such tradition in the early twentieth century among the Kwakiutl (more properly known as the Kwak'waka'wakw), where individuals celebrating their salmon spirit power donned salmon masks and danced, leaping upward like salmon leap when they are spawning. By enacting this movement, dancers undertake a spiritual journey to the undersea world of the salmon people, where they affirm in spirit their relationship with and dependence on them. The salmon people themselves respond in kind the following spring, summer, and fall, by donning their own salmon masks and swimming upstream to their spawning grounds. Such dances reenact and affirm the people's relationship to the salmon people through the very act of transformation first seen in the Northwest Coast creation stories.[16] In such winter ceremonials as this, people symbolically become animals, moving between states of being as they dance. In the months of fishing or hunting, the animal people are transformed as well, taking on their animal flesh to become food for the people of the Northwest Coast.[17]

Similar traditions of transformation are recognized within First Salmon ceremonies. As already mentioned in Chapter 1, Coast Salish oral traditions describe the salmon as people, like the Coast Salish themselves, although these are people who live in an undersea village, who wear the cloaks of salmon flesh, and who have the ability to die and be reborn year after year. While Coast Salish people fish for, catch, and eat salmon, they also recognize the salmon to be more spiritually powerful than themselves. In order to assure that the salmon people will continue to return each year, giving themselves to the Salish, the Coast Salish know that they must honor their ancestral relationship with the salmon, receive them as honored guests, and speak to them with respect. On the Northwest Coast, traditional stories abound of individuals who treated the salmon disrespectfully, damaged relationships irreparably, and caused the salmon never to return to a particular river.

Another illustration of this theme of transformation and the ability to journey between worlds is the Coast Salish Spirit Canoe ceremony, a healing rite intended to retrieve a patient's soul that has wandered away.[18] Jay Miller has published two books on this subject, in which he discusses the ceremony and its role in Coast Salish healing.[19] In its full form, the ceremony is enacted through the cooperation of several spiritual leaders, who make use of planks and effigies to create a virtual "canoe." In a trance state, these spiritual elders journey to the land of the dead to retrieve this lost soul. This ceremony is undertaken during the winter months, both because this is the time when winter ceremonial syó'wən dances are held, and because when it is winter in the land of the living, it is summer in the land of the dead.

According to Miller, a space would be cleared in the center of the floor, creating a middle aisle lined by paired planks. Effigies belonging to the spiritual practitioners are placed between them. These spiritual specialists then call on their various guardian spirits to assist them in their journey. Planks are cut and painted to represent the spiritual entities present. The planks are covered in white paint and black outlines, on which each practitioner has formed images of his or her guardian spirit in red, black, and white paint. Other poles are carved and painted to represent the tools they may need along their journey, such as arrows, spears, and paddles. When the ceremony begins, the ritual specialists sing their spirit power songs, inviting their guardian spirits to be present. Such spirits rush to the longhouse, taking up residence within the painted effigy, and accompanying the singers on their travels. The spiritual leaders then undertake this harrowing journey, moving through a variety of trials and adventures, acquiring power and food, overcoming dangerous attackers, and moving into the land of the spirits. The singers arrive at the land of the dead and undertake a fierce battle for the patient's lost soul. Having secured the spirit, they bring it back with them, again through a harrowing journey, bringing it to the patient who has been resting at the back of the house. The soul is poured back into the patient, who slowly recovers, singing her or his spirit song. On their return, these spiritual practitioners are able to offer healing to other individuals, or to promise wealth and success in hunting or gathering. Planks and other paraphernalia from the dance are carried into the woods, and left there to decay naturally, although spiritual practitioners keep the effigies of their guardian spirits, carefully maintaining them throughout their lives. The Spirit Canoe dance has not been enacted in its full form for nearly a century. However, smaller versions of this ceremony are still enacted today within curing ceremonies.

Ceremonial activities such as the vision quests, winter ceremonials, First Salmon ceremonies, and the Spirit Canoe ceremony, as well as the ritual paraphernalia that accompanied them (such as rattles, masks, crests, and house posts), are all modes through which spiritual power is concentrated and brought within the human community, and through which the spiritual principle of transformation is embodied within ritual activity. As in oral traditions about Transformer, or Changer, the lines between human and the more-than-human communities are thin and frequently crossed. Within traditional Coast Salish ceremonials, animals and humans are able symbolically and ontologically to change from one to the other by donning a mask and undertaking a spiritual journey, thus participating in the ritual processes of transformation.

Foundations of Diné traditions

Before the arrival of Europeans in the American Southwest, the Diné lived alongside their Pueblo neighbors in relative peace, caring for their corn fields, hunting, and (from the nineteenth century) raising sheep. As with the Lakota and the Coast Salish, Diné spirituality emerged from the unique landscape in which they lived; to the four mountain ranges that border the Diné homeland in the American Southwest can be attributed the reverence for rain in an arid climate and the Diné reliance on corn and sheep for their food and clothing. These mountains are the home of the ye'ii, the Holy People responsible for the creation of the Diné cosmos. Diné origin stories reflect the people's agricultural lifestyle: the Holy People emerge from the earth, just as corn emerges from the earth after planting. The Diné themselves are created from earth, their bodies formed from corn and minerals, molded together by Changing Woman. Underlying Diné cosmology is the notion of *Nilch'i*, sometimes defined as Holy Wind, which animates and binds the cosmos. The heart of Diné ceremonialism and religion is, in many ways, about negotiating and balancing *Nilch'i*.

Diné emergence[20]

At the beginning, the Diné Holy People ascended through three levels of the underworld before reaching this one. The first level was black, the second blue, the third yellow, and the fourth (this earth) white. According to one account of creation related by James K. McNeley, creation began when light "misted up" from the four horizons: White Early Dawn (*hayołkááł*) in the east; Blue Sky Noon (*nahodeeł'iizh*) in the south; Yellow Sunset (*nahootsoii*) in the west; and Dark Night (*chahałheeł*) in the north. These mists were the inner forms of the cardinal directions, and the inner forms of the mountains that mark them. From these four directions likewise came *Nilch'i*, Holy Wind. *Nilch'i* came in the form of winds, which gave life and power to the inhabitants of the first world: First Man, First Woman, and the Holy People or *ye'ii*. *Nilch'i* supplied the living with breath, thought, and understanding.[21]

A series of cataclysms drove the Holy People to ascend from first one world to the next, from black world, to yellow world, to blue world. In the third world, however, the *Diyin Diyinii* argued with each other. Men and women began to think that they could do without each other, believing that they were sufficient on their own. They quarreled, and men and women determined to live apart from each other, on opposite sides of a river. But living so long apart, their sexual desire increased. The women sought to satisfy themselves with long stones, thick quills, cactus, bone, or corn; men with mud or raw meat. Eventually the people realized that the genders were meant to be together, working cooperatively. They reunited, aware that they needed each other for happiness and children.[22]

Shortly thereafter a great flood forced the Holy People to ascend to this world, at the Place of Emergence. There First Man and First Woman built a sweat house and sang the new world into being. First Man opened his mountain soil bundle, which contained soil from the four directions of the underworlds. From this bundle, he built the first *hooghan* as model of the new world to come. The *hooghan* had four pillars at the four directions. The round floor marked out the round space of the earth, while the round ceiling symbolized the sky. The door at the east, First Man determined, was the place of birth and beginning.

The *Diyin Diyinii* gathered together in the *hooghan*, and First Man expanded it to make it large enough for all the Holy People. Within this first *hooghan*, he set in place the four directions and the mountains that marked them. First Man and First Woman determined the seven directions that would define the Diné world: the four cardinal directions, zenith (top), nadir (bottom), and center. To mark the directions they located the six mountains: in the east, Blanca Peak (*Sisnaajinii*); in the south, Mount Taylor (*Tsoodził*); in the west, San Francisco Peaks (*Dook'o'oostłííd*); in the north, La Plata Peak (*Dibé Ntsaa*); and in the center, Huerfano Peak and Gobernador Knob.

First Man then assigned each of the *Diyin Diyinii* to stand as the inner forms within each mountain and within each plant, animal, and mineral that lived on the mountains. He assigned them as couples, male and female, to live in the cardinal directions. To the east, he sent Early Dawn Boy and Early Dawn Girl; to the south, Blue Daylight Boy and Blue Daylight Girl. To the west, he sent Yellow Evening Twilight Boy and Yellow Evening Twilight Girl; and to the North, Folding Darkness Boy and Folding Darkness Girl. These Holy People became the inner forms of the mountains, and they were adorned with the minerals of those mountains: white shell, turquoise, abalone, and jet.[23]

To animate this new world, to bring it into motion and movement, First Man sent out Holy Winds.[24] These winds moved through all things, through stones, minerals, plants, and animals, animating and giving breath to everything on the earth. He assigned Holy Wind messengers to the pairs of Holy People, to act as messengers, to carry the Holy People's thoughts and intentions throughout the earth and to each other. First Man then dressed the four mountains. He pinned Blanca Peak to the earth with a bolt of lightning and he dressed it in white: white shell, morning light, white lightning, white rain, dark clouds, and white corn. Mount Taylor was pinned to the earth with a great stone knife and dressed in blue: turquoise, dark mist, daylight, blue corn, and wild animals. San Francisco Peak was held to the earth with a sunbeam, and dressed in yellow: abalone shell, sunset, blue clouds, yellow cord, and animals. La Plata Peak was bound to the earth with a rainbow and dressed in black: jet, night, dark mist, plants, and animals. Then First Man and First Woman created the sun, moon, sky, winds, constellations, and seasons. They established birth and death and gave names to the animals. The world was set in perfect order, harmony, and balance: a state of *hozho*.

Although the world began in order and beauty, disorder and ugliness were soon introduced. Monsters roamed the earth, killing healthy babies and causing the Holy People to become infertile. This world was in *nichxo'i*: ugliness, disorder, chaos, sickness, imbalance, and infertility. *Nichxo'i* emerged into the world first when the Holy People had briefly forgotten their dependence on each other; they had forgotten the need for masculine and feminine to come together and care for each other, and for the balance of powers.

Things looked dire until one day First Man was out walking and discovered Changing Woman. She was raised by First Man and First Woman and grew up in twelve days. At her first menstruation, the first *Kinààldá* was performed. Soon Changing Woman was impregnated by the sun and gave birth to twin sons: Monster Slayer and Child of the Water. Her twins grew quickly and became great warriors, who rid the world of monsters. When the world was safe, Changing Woman took some of her flesh and molded it together with the four colors of corn and the four minerals from the four directions: white, blue, yellow, and black, and white shell, turquoise, abalone shell, and jet. She shaped the concoction into human form and created the first earth people, the Diné. The human form was animated by Holy Winds, *Nilch'i*, which entered the body from the four directions, through the swirls on the tips of its toes and fingers, through the swirls of its ears, through the top of its head.

Diné notions of power

Within the Diné cosmology, **Sa'a Naaghai Bik'eh Hozho** is a central philosophical concept, influencing traditional notions of the sacred. Difficult to translate or define, it is a synthesis of the entire Navajo religious and philosophical system. Some scholars have translated it as "Long Life-Happiness." Others translate it as, "According to the Ideal May Restoration Be Achieved." Still other scholars have pointed out that *Sa'a Naaghai Bik'eh Hozho* suggests the interaction of male and female principles of creation. According to John Farella, *Sa'a Naaghai* suggests a masculine energy, while *Bik'eh Hozho* suggests a feminine one.[25] This philosophical ideal seems to suggest an animating energy, one of rejuvenation, reanimation, fertility, and creation. Male and female energies exist in tandem, each mutually dependent on the other, different but equally crucial parts of a vital whole. It is because of *Sa'a Naaghai* and *Bik'eh Hozho* that the universe continues to reproduce and to exist in balance, and that male and female beings continue to be drawn to each other.[26] This spiritual principle is responsible for rainfall, the fertility of the earth, the growth of corn, the vitality of livestock, human reproduction, and cultural strength. Corn, the primary food staple of the traditional Diné, occupies a central place within Diné ritual activity and symbolism. As shown in the ceremony described in Chapter 1, corn pollen, embodying the fertility and potential for growth inherent in the cosmos, was and is a central aspect of Diné ceremony.

The creative power in the Diné universe thus binds human and spiritual communities together. Individuals are tied to their partners, their communities, their ancestors, First Man and First Woman, Changing Woman, the present and the future, the earth, the heavens, and the four directions. To recognize and cultivate this creative energy within oneself is to recognize one's origins in the cosmos and one's interrelatedness with the Diné landscape, its ancestors, and the Holy People. To grow in spiritual maturity is to realize one's interconnectedness and kinship with the universe. According to an interpretation put forth by Farella, *Sa'a Naaghai Bik'eh Hozho*, male–female energies in complementarity, is completeness. It emerges from the four directions and is a vehicle for increase, reproduction, and sexuality, for the realization of the interconnectedness of the universe: these energies and their realization enable one to live a long, healthy, creative, and constantly renewing life.

Nilch'i, Holy Wind, distributed and set in place by First Man during the formative era of this earth, also acts as a powerful animating force in traditional Diné philosophy. Winds inflate, give strength, motion, and change; they give life to animals, plants, people, mountains, water, stones, and soil. As the primary energy in the universe, wind is creator, life giver, and sustainer. Winds give direction to living things; they give movement, the ability to think, and the motion to carry out what needs to be done. While there is one essential Holy Wind, it is expressed and found in many different forms: the winds of the four directions that reside in the mountains and provide knowledge and breath to the Holy People; winds that animate the earth, water, and clouds; and various minor winds with destructive or precocious properties, such as Sunward Revolving Wind, Coiled Wind, Striped Wind, Wavy Back Wind. The same winds that first animated Changing Woman, bringing her to life, animate the Diné people and all that surrounds them.

The nature of Holy Winds, both as an animating force and as a messenger of the Holy People, makes them a vital part of Diné spirituality and ceremony. As messengers between the inner forms of earth and sky, the winds monitor, guide, and direct human life. Winds and Holy People reside in all living things; they are the life, breath, movement, and speech of earth and living things on it. Inappropriate human thoughts or actions are instantly related to the Holy People by these messenger winds. Offending the Holy People, or Holy Winds, results in the wind's withdrawing from a person.

Just like Changing Woman herself, so the Diné are animated and given life by Holy Winds. Winds move the body on a physiological level, animating blood vessels, muscles, and organ systems. Winds also motivate the body on a spiritual and intellectual level, guiding clarity of thought, will to action, emotions, and spiritual balance. When these winds withdraw from the body, sickness or death can result. As one scholar describes it: "According to the Navajo conception ... winds exist all around and within the individual, entering and departing through respiratory organs and whorls on the body's surface. That which is within and that which surrounds one is all the same and it is holy."[27] The focus of much Diné ceremony thus works to restore a healthy interaction with Holy Winds, by establishing good and balanced relationships with the Holy People and inner forms of the cosmos. To be healthy is to be in a state of *Sa'a Naaghai Bik'eh Hozho*, to reflect and mirror the harmonious nature of the universe. As one Diné elder explains it, "The same wind moves us ... you see, the same Wind's Child exists within our tissues, it moves us, it causes us to think."[28] The same Holy Wind that brought the universe into creation moved the earth, animates water, and moves the internal self.

Much of Diné spirituality centers on the performance of chant-ways, ceremonies that cure individuals of physio-spiritual ailments and restore them to a balanced and harmonious relationship with the Diné landscape and the *Diyin Diyinii* that reside within it. Traditional Diné ceremonialism thus developed as a means of bringing the individual back into a state of *Sa'a Naaghai Bik'eh Hozho*. Chantways, such as the Blessingway, or *Nizhoni,* are complex ceremonial sings taking from one to nine days, and are held in a ceremonial *hooghan.* Each has its origin in a sacred story: a hero or heroine undertakes a journey and meets Holy People, who teach a ceremony, including the songs, prayers, and sand paintings that should accompany them. The hero or heroine then returns, teaching the chantway to his or her people.[29]

One central element of a chantway is the creation of sand paint-ings, complex dry paintings with images of the four directions, the four mountains, and the Holy People. The patient sits in the center of the painting, while the medicine man or woman tells the hero's journey in song and prayer. The presence of the Holy People is invoked, and the individual is restored to balance through their presence. These chantways strengthen good winds, remove negative winds, and help the individual relocate him- or herself within the Diné sacred geography. Through the chantways the individual remembers who he or she is, and where he or she came from. Such ceremonies are not simply symbolic recreations of sacred stories. Rather, through speech and ritual embodiment of the stories, Holy Winds are brought back into balance, and human and spiritual relationships are restored. The patient is brought back to a state of *Sa'a Naaghai Bik'eh Hozho*: beauty, harmony, order, balance, well-being.

Conclusion

The three traditions discussed in this chapter illustrate the diver-sity of Native religious life. Origin stories, notions of power, and ceremonial ways of negotiating spiritual power differ dramatically. These differences reflect the vast differences of the ecosystems within which the traditions emerged, for each is, first and foremost, an autochthonous tradition, emerging from a people's relationship with the landscape that nurtures and sustains them: the Northern Plains and Black Hills; the temperate coastal rain forest of the Pacific Northwest; and the high mountainous deserts of the Diné homeland. However, these three traditions also demonstrate key similarities. They share a sense of spiritual power as depending on the cultivation of reciprocal relationships with spirits within the landscape. None of these communities sees spirituality as a compartmentalized part of life, but rather each one integrates spirituality into its daily activities, from fishing, to farming, to cooking, to dreaming. Finally, as each tradition emerges from a particular landscape, it exists in relationship with that landscape and with the indigenous foods that that landscape provided: bison, salmon, or corn.

The arrival of Europeans in North America heralded a dramatic shift in indigenous life on this continent, irrevocably changing the shape of Native culture and society. Europeans brought with them new technologies, new faiths, and new pathogens that would have a profound impact on Native communities. This chapter presents a brief overview of American Indian religious history since 1608, when Euroamerican missions to North America began. It charts the course  of federal policies and missionary agendas from the earliest missions of the French Jesuits in New France to the Termination and Relocation policies of the 1950s and '60s. Painting with broad strokes, I seek to demonstrate two opposing trends within United States Indian policies: coerced assimilation and cultural preservation. The second half of the chapter goes on to describe indigenous Americans' response to and experience of these policies and agendas. In keeping with the overall format of this book, the Lakota, the Coast Salish, and the Diné are each discussed in detail. In short, this chapter outlines the processes of colonization, proselytization, and assimilation that assaulted Native people over four centuries and the creative, resilient ways in which Native communities rose to meet these threats.

Throughout the seventeenth and eighteenth centuries, colonial efforts at assimilation were primarily expressed through missionary efforts. Such efforts operated within a historical moment of discovery, when European colonial powers were determining their New World borders and establishing the role that each was to have in North America. Relationships between European and Native nations were key factors in the political and economic maneuvering between Spanish, French, and British interests, and those of American colonists in the New World, as each group sought to use Native alliances to gain power in military and political battles. Missionaries worked within the existing political context, laboring to secure converts to their particular brand of Christianity and, in the process, to procure political allies for their own government. However, with the conclusion of the Revolutionary War and the War of 1812, Europe's stake in North America was largely settled: the borders had been drawn. From this point, relations between Euroamericans and Native Americans changed dramatically, as the focus shifted away from concerns of foreign policy and toward a new United States' national policy that emphasized the ideal of a homogenous cohesive nation, unified within a single language and culture.[1] From the Euroamerican perspective within this newly forming United States, there were three options for the Native Americans: termination, assimilation, or removal.

1812–1960: Termination, assimilation, and removal

Federal lawmakers espousing policies of assimilation in the early nineteenth century argued that Native people could be taught to live like Europeans. The goal, still in keeping with early English Protestant agendas, was for the full-scale "civilization" and incorporation of Native people into Euroamerican society. As early as 1819, Congress established the Indian Civilization Fund Act, appropriating funds to teach Native people farming and animal husbandry, and to educate them toward citizenship. Such policies were not as benign as they may seem, however, for in every case of monies expended, assimilationist policies were directly tied to efforts to secure more Native-owned land for Euroamerican settlement. These assimilationist policies always existed alongside political agendas aimed at the outright removal or termination of Native people. For many policy makers, the displacement of indigenous communities was the first logical step toward Euroamerican expansion. As European settlements in the northeast grew, Native nations were systematically pushed farther and farther west.[2]

The history of the Cherokee people presents a striking illustration of the tension between United States Indian policies of assimilation and removal. As early as the mid-eighteenth century, the Cherokee were a model of assimilationist ideals. They had developed a sedentary agricultural society, lived in wood-frame houses, and had structured their governance and economy along an English model. By 1817, the Cherokee had established their nation as a republic, with a legislature, a supreme court, European-style law enforcement, and a system of taxation. To imitate the embryonic United States, they abandoned their age-old practice of equality for women. They welcomed Protestant mission schools, developed a distinctly Cherokee writing system, and in 1829 founded the *Cherokee Phoenix*, the newspaper of the Cherokee nation. By this time, the Cherokee were successful farmers and slave holders; they had constructed roads, ferries, schools, and churches. Such assimilating efforts were made, in part, as a conscious effort to stave off the threat of removal to which many other Native nations had fallen prey. In many ways they were a perfect example of what assimilationist lawmakers hoped to achieve. They varied, however, in one very important respect: they retained their national sovereignty and their historic homeland. In 1829, Andrew Jackson became President, and gold was discovered in northern Georgia. As a result, in 1830, Congress signed into law the Indian Removal Bill. Choctaws, Chickasaws, and Creeks were removed west, and part of the Seminole followed in 1832, after struggling to hold Euroamerican forces off in a bloody and inconclusive war. In 1838, following a controversial removal agreement signed by a minority of their leadership, the Cherokee were forcibly removed to Indian Territory (now Oklahoma), a tragically destructive journey during which one quarter of their people died. This period of removal has since become known as the Trail of Tears.[3]

Cherokee removal demonstrated the inherent inconsistency of assimilationist policies, for even the seemingly almost perfectly assimilated Cherokee were no match for Euroamerican demands for land and mineral development. This instance, and many others that followed, illustrate that even those federal policies originally formulated with good intentions were complicated by deeply held convictions that Native people must ultimately be removed from the land, opening the country to Euroamerican control. The goal of nearly every federal policy, whether for removal or assimilation, has tended toward the cultural, and at times physical, elimination of Native people.

This is further illustrated by the decades of expansion that followed. During this time, large numbers of Euroamericans traveled west in search of land, as did Native nations that had been displaced from their homes in the east. This westward expansion prompted widespread violence across the western frontier as Native nations resisted encroachment on their territory. By 1850, the United States army had forced most Native communities onto reservations, many of which had negotiated treaties with the federal government to protect certain rights and access to traditional subsistence resources. These reservations disrupted indigenous religious life in countless ways. Indigenous traditions had their roots in sacred spaces within their traditional landbase. Locked into reservations, Native people lost access to many of their most important sacred sites, including essential locations in which they traditionally conducted ceremonies and to which they went for vision quests. In return for moving onto reservations, Native people were promised food, clothing, housing, medical care, and education—in the language of the treaties, "all goods and services necessary for civilization." But such supplies often did not arrive. Government agents often misappropriated funds and rations, redirecting them for their own profit. In the mid- to late nineteenth century, Native people confined to reservations faced starvation, escalating rates of disease, inadequate medical care, and a lack of proper clothing or housing.

Seeing the poverty, violence, and neglect produced by the reservation system, federal reformers began to call for an end to the segregation of reservation life. They insisted that (despite what was promised in treaties) reservations had been intentionally designed as temporary locations for Native people while they underwent the assimilation process. The reformers argued that assimilation was the only hope for Native people, and that it would, conveniently, open up reservation land to Euroamerican settlement. President Grant's 1869 Peace Policy was developed to safeguard this Euroamerican expansion west by promoting the assimilation of tribes living in lands desired by settlers. Grant established as a Board of Indian Commissioners a group of Christian laymen, and he assigned them to monitor officials from the Bureau of Indian Affairs (BIA) and recommend appointments to agency posts.[4] Missionaries, Grant reasoned, would be less likely to seek monetary benefit or to rob the people they were appointed to serve, and would simultaneously be responsible for political leadership, distribution of rations, medical care, and the task of civilizing the Indians. Grant's administration established a system of boarding schools, convinced that they were the most expedient and effective way of educating students into English, Christianity, and the virtues of Western education. On numerous reservations, children were forcibly removed from their homes and communities; often they were not allowed to return for years. The traditional family structure of tribes was torn apart. The Peace Policy, although initiated as an effort to reform a troubled system, ultimately failed.[5] This was due in part to the appointment of inexperienced missionaries to agency posts, but also to the aggressive encroachment of white settlers into Indian Territory. The system's firm assimilationist stance left no room for indigenous leadership, culture, or sovereignty, and thus did little to appeal to indigenous communities.

As the reservation system continued to decline in the late nineteenth century, reformers became convinced that the system itself perpetuated poverty and social marginalization. As before, the goal for such reformers was to lead Native people to civilization, Christianity, and citizenship. As these reformers saw it, the first obstacle to this process was not lack of education, but indigenous traditions of communally held land. Private property, agricultural economies, and participation in a capitalist system of exchange were vital, these Euroamerican reformers claimed, for the survival of Native people in a changing world.[6] As James McLaughlin, the Indian Agent who would later arrest Sitting Bull, argued, the best one could do for "the Indian" was to "give him his portion and turn him loose to work out his own salvation."[7] In 1882, Thomas Morgan sought to further this assimilation effort by establishing the BIA's *Rules of Indian Courts*. The *Rules* encouraged Indian Agents to put an end to any indigenous ritual activity or gathering, and it provided for a punishment of thirty days in prison, or six months for a medicine man conducting such a gathering, in line with the BIA policy of ensuring that Native people "abandon and discontinue medicine practices."[8] In 1922, Commissioner Charles Burke continued the federal government's policy of enforced assimilation when he issued Circular 1665, which strongly advised agents to act to prohibit traditional religious practices and gatherings. If communal land ownership was the first obstacle to assimilation, the second was thus Native religion, for reformers were convinced that civilization required Christianization.

The Dawes or General Allotment Act of 1887 (authored by Congressman Henry Dawes) accomplished both goals. First, it promoted the effort to break up indigenous communitarian land ownership, in the process freeing more land for white settlement. A family would receive a 160-acre allotment; an individual over age eighteen could receive 80 acres; those who received an allotment would eventually (after a twenty-five-year trust period) be able to petition for citizenship. Any "surplus" land left over after allotments were made would become open for Euroamerican settlement. As a result of the Dawes Act, between 1887 and 1934, 60% of reservation land was taken as "surplus" after allotments were made and was opened for settlement.[9] Second, the act made a firm statement against the practice of traditional religion, and the government made a renewed effort to place Native children in Christian boarding schools. The policy thus met two popular demands of Euroamerican society: assimilation and land acquisition.

Some reformers of the Dawes Act era envisioned Native people gradually moving into Euroamerican society, finally vanishing into the melting pot created by Protestantism and western European values. Government officials, however, soon became frustrated at the lack of success in their assimilationist programs, and felt it necessary to extend greater control over indigenous religious and cultural life. This included increased federal control over Native lands and natural resources. When citizenship was finally granted to all Native Americans in 1924, federal officials made it clear that the decision in no way changed the position of Native people as wards of the state. They were treated as minors, whose interests were to be overseen by the paternalistic eye of the federal government. By the end of the 1920s, assimilation had come to mean something very different than it had in the 1870s. Rather than being a means of entry into Euroamerican society as equals, assimilation policies of the late nineteenth and early twentieth centuries sought only to create a docile working class, laboring on individual plots of land under the stewardship and control of the federal government.

In 1933, at a time when Native life was characterized by extreme poverty, landlessness, poor education, and vastly inadequate healthcare, Franklin Roosevelt appointed John Collier as Commissioner of Indian Affairs. Collier sought to promote the protection of indigenous spiritual and cultural traditions, the recovery of lost reservation land, and the return of self-rule to Native communities. His first task was to abolish the Board of Indian Commissioners, which he saw as aggressively promoting the assimilation of Native people and cultures. In his 1934 Indian Reorganization Act (also known as the Wheeler–Howard Act), Collier restored local governance to tribal nations, ended compulsory attendance in government boarding schools (many of which were religiously affiliated), did away with the allotment system, worked to consolidate checkerboard reservations and restore unallotted land to tribes, reorganized the school system, and provided scholarships for higher education. In addition, he overturned the ban on Native American religious practice. Collier's work did much to improve the political, cultural, and spiritual survival of Native people. The act was nevertheless problematic in that it worked to recreate tribal governance along a Euroamerican model rather than maintaining traditional systems of authority.[10] Despite its shortcomings, however, Collier's reforms succeeded in many ways, particularly because they placed control and autonomy back in the hands of Native people and encouraged the preservation of traditional cultures.

Collier's work was challenged during the 1950s, when federal policy again took a conservative turn, emphasizing the assimilationist goals of earlier generations. This policy, often referred to as "Termination and Relocation," emphasized ending social services to Native communities, abolishing tribal status, and integrating Native people into the urban laboring classes. Once again determining that reservations and tribal governments were preventing the assimilation of Native people into the dominant society, federal agencies terminated the tribal status of many Nations and worked to relocate Native people to urban centers such as Minnesota, Los Angeles, Phoenix, Dallas, Chicago, and Seattle. The effort was a disaster for many Native people, who found themselves cut off from their families and communities. Having been promised jobs and economic success by the government, many of them arrived in cities to find poverty and cultural isolation. Even though the Termination and Relocation policies were short-lived, some communities whose tribal status was terminated in the 1950s and '60s are still fighting to regain federal recognition of their existence as a nation.

As the above examples demonstrate, federal policies maintained three common priorities throughout their history: the assimilation of Native people into Euroamerican society and religion; the suppression of indigenous spiritual and cultural traditions; and the removal of Native people from their land. Alongside such policies were the efforts of some reformers and missionaries to ensure the survival of Native people, but, with the brief exception of Collier's reforms, this entire history is marked by an overarching assimilationist agenda, one that denied Native nations sovereignty and control over their own political and cultural destinies.

Indigenous responses: Reconstructing religious and cultural life

As living conditions on Native reservations worsened, so indigenous resistance grew. This resistance frequently expressed itself within religious movements. As early as the 1860s, government officials, committed to the goals of cultural assimilation, had responded to such resistance with legislation restricting the practice of Native religious ceremonies and gatherings. In 1883, the United States government passed the Indian Religious Crimes code, imposing prison sentences and suspending rations for Native people caught leading or participating in indigenous ceremonies. Many missionary efforts during this time met with great success, but others encountered staunch resistance. Even though each community had a unique relationship with the missionaries that approached it, several common issues often arose that complicated evangelistic efforts.

Ideologically and theologically, Christianity and indigenous religions tended to disagree on several fundamental ideas. First was the notion of sin. For Christians, right and wrong were determined by divine mandate and recorded in a changeless book; committing a sin was an offence against an all-powerful God. For Native people, however, right and wrong generally were dictated by the needs of the community. Actions that promoted harmony and community well-being were positive; actions that created discord were negative. The notion of Original Sin only complicated missionary efforts. While most Christians taught that human nature was inherently flawed and naturally depraved, most Native communities saw people as naturally good, that is, inclined toward balance and right action. Monotheism, as taught by Christianity, also seemed strange to Native peoples, especially as it seemed to be contradicted by the Christian doctrine of the Trinity. While some indigenous communities had a notion of a creator, or of a pervasive animating spirit, their spiritual traditions and notions of the sacred were quite different from the anthropomorphic monotheism of Christianity. But a greater obstacle to conversion and assimilation than theology was the degree to which Christianity alienated an individual from her or his community, family, and extended kinship network. Culturally and religiously, Native identity depended on being part of a wider tribal community. Conversion often meant a cruel break with the web of relationships that defined one's very sense of self.[11]

Rather than embrace wholesale conversion, Native communities generally responded in one of three ways: some joined the church and attempted to assimilate; some joined revitalistic movements meant to return the people to a traditional life; while others creatively navigated these new traditions in other ways, revitalizing their cultures through a selected use of Christian and Euroamerican beliefs and practices, and taking only those European cultural elements necessary for survival. In the northeast, for instance, revitalistic movements emerged as early as 1800. Seneca prophet Sganyadai:yo, or Handsome Lake, came forward at a time when his people were in crisis. Having sided with the British in the Revolutionary War, his people had lost considerable political power when the war ended in favor of American colonists. Materially and culturally the people were at a crisis point. Handsome Lake called for the revival of traditional religious and cultural practices and for the rejection of destructive influences such as alcohol, witchcraft, suicide, and despair. He also founded the Gaiwiio, or Longhouse religion, which is still practiced today.[12] Similarly, the Shawnee Tenskwatawa, brother of the famous Tecumseh, rose to prominence in 1805, calling for spiritual reform, a return to traditional life, and a rejection of Euroamerican influences such as intermarriage and alcohol.[13]

Despite the best assimilationist efforts of the United States government, military, and missionaries, Native religious traditions survived. While maintaining core spiritual beliefs, principles, and symbols, indigenous traditions adapted in creative ways to meet new needs and new challenges. The remainder of this chapter turns once again to the three nations under consideration throughout this book—the Lakota, the Coast Salish, and the Diné—to explore how specific nations experienced and responded to the tumultuous centuries of colonial conquest.

The Lakota: The Ghost Dance

Before the mid-nineteenth century, the Lakota flourished in the Northern Plains. However, with the arrival of Euroamerican settlers came devastating diseases, many of which spread faster than the settlers themselves, traveling from tribe to tribe with fierce speed. Settlers on their way to Oregon and the gold rush in California brought additional waves of cholera, smallpox, and measles that devastated Lakota communities. As settlers dispersed game and trespassed on Native land, the Lakota began a decades-long war against these Euroamericans, challenging their right to cross Lakota territory.

Warfare increased between the Lakota and the United States Army, until the United States and the Lakota signed the Fort Laramie Treaty in 1868.[14] The treaty established the Great Sioux Reservation: the entire region of South Dakota west of the Missouri River, including the Black Hills. Hunting rights were recognized within the treaty, as well as a region of Unceded Territory set aside for material sustenance. This territory included northwest Nebraska, northeast Wyoming, and southwest Montana east of the Big Horn Mountains. According to the treaty, the Great Sioux Reservation was "set apart for the absolute and undisturbed use and occupation of the Indians herein named." However, the treaty was soon broken. Euroamerican settlers continued to trespass on Native land, and United States officials led railroad-surveying teams into Lakota land. Such surveys were illegal. As conflict escalated, the United States government formulated a policy of exterminating the bison, arguing, as General Sherman, Commander of U.S. forces in the West, did before Congress in March of 1873, "kill the bison, and you kill the Indians." When, in 1873 and 1874, General George Armstrong Custer led illegal railroad- and gold-prospecting surveys into the Black Hills, the Lakota were outraged.

After Custer's discovery of gold in the Black Hills was widely publicized, Euroamerican gold miners poured into the region. By 1875, 15,000 Euroamerican gold miners had taken up residency in the Black Hills in direct violation of the 1868 treaty. In 1876, the United States Department of War ordered all Lakota to be confined to the reservation. When some Lakota leaders, including Sitting Bull and Crazy Horse, refused to follow this order, Custer and his men were dispatched to bring such renegade bands forcibly within reservation boundaries. This period of conflict culminated in the Battle of Little Big Horn and the defeat of Custer's 7th Cavalry. Hence, within less than a decade of signing the 1868 treaty, the buffalo had been brought nearly to extinction, gold had been discovered in the Black Hills, the famous battle with Custer had been fought, and the original treaty had been disregarded to allow Euroamerican gold prospectors into the region.

Later, when the Dawes Act was implemented on the Great Sioux Reservation, Lakota land was reduced by more than 50%. Forced onto a diminishing reservation, restricted from access to their traditional hunting grounds, and faced with the near extermination of the bison, the Lakota people suffered from high rates of illness, starvation, and lack of resources. Promised rations from the United States government were slow to arrive, and when they did they were often sorely inadequate. High mortality rates meant that nearly every family had suffered losses, and every community struggled with the deaths of respected elders and young children.

Against this historical backdrop, many of the Lakota turned to a new revitalistic religious movement: the Ghost Dance. The dance originated in 1889, when Wovoka, a Paiute also known by his English name Jack Wilson, experienced a series of visions in which he died and was taken to heaven, where he was given a message to deliver to the Indian people. The people must dance a circle dance, and sing the songs that they received in visions. If they did so, their dead would return, led by a returning Christ. Jesus had come once before, Wovoka taught, but white people killed him; now he was coming back for the Indians. The world was going to be transformed. All would be swept away, but the faithful who believed and danced would be saved. The whites would all be gone, the buffalo would return, and the old ways of life would be restored. Dancers were to abandon modern dress and return to traditional modes of living. Wovoka also taught that Native people were to lead moral, ethical lives, having faith that Christ would soon return.

The Ghost Dance spread rapidly throughout the Great Plains and as far west as California. Two Minniconjou spiritual leaders, Kicking Bear and Short Bull, brought the Ghost Dance to the Lakota. It was in the midst of Ghost Dances that both Black Elk and Kicking Bear had visions of Ghost Dance shirts, which, according to some interpretations, when painted with symbols from Ghost Dance visions, would protect faithful Lakota dancers from gunfire. The dance and the powerful shirts spread quickly throughout the Lakota reservations, providing both an outlet for grief at their many losses, and a means of spiritual cohesion and reviving threatened traditions.[15]

The Indian Agent administering Pine Ridge, however, viewed the dance as a dangerous threat. Agent P.F. Wells wrote to James McLaughlin, U.S. Indian Agent at Standing Rock Reservation, on October 19, 1890: "If you can nab him [Kicking Bear] before he can get them started you will save yourself no end of trouble. I say this because you or anyone else can have no idea how bad it takes hold of the Indians as some of our best Indians are nearly crazy over it."[16] Fearful of another uprising, Indian Agents sought to arrest Ghost Dance leaders. On December 15, 1890, tribal police attempted to arrest the spiritual leader Sitting Bull. A struggle ensued, and Sitting Bull was killed.

On hearing the news of Sitting Bull's death, Big Foot, another Lakota tribal leader, determined to lead his people south to Pine Ridge for safety and supplies. He and his band of 350 were intercepted along the way by the U.S. Army's 7th Cavalry, the unit the Lakota had defeated at Little Big Horn. The cavalry directed the group to stop for the night at Wounded Knee, and the soldiers set up camp on a rise surrounding the people. Big Foot and his people complied. What happened the next morning, December 29, is debated, but according to many accounts a disruption occurred while a soldier was attempting to disarm a man who may have been deaf. The man's rifle fired, and at the sound the cavalry opened fire, including four Hotchkiss guns, on the group of civilians. Within a few minutes more than 300 people, most of them women and children, had been killed. Twenty-five soldiers were also killed by friendly fire. Although there were other instances of

Black Elk was an important spiritual leader to his Lakota people, serving them as medicine man, ceremonial leader, and Catholic catechist. Gifted with a powerful vision in his early childhood, Black Elk devoted his life to guiding his people through the painful transition of the colonial era.

extreme violence, such as those against the Cheyenne and Blackfeet, the massacre at Wounded Knee soon became a symbol of U.S. brutality against Native people.[17]

The spiritual leader Black Elk lived throughout this tumultuous period of Lakota history. He was five years old when the 1868 Fort Laramie Treaty was signed, and he witnessed the massacre at Wounded Knee. In his early childhood, Black Elk became very ill and had a powerful vision that instructed him to lead his people through the transitional years ahead and to work for a renewal of Lakota culture. The vision was recorded and put into poetic verse by John G. Neihardt in his book *Black Elk Speaks*.

Black Elk is a remarkable example of this era of Native history, particularly for the way in which he responded to the dual pressures of cultural preservation and assimilation that characterized the late nineteenth and early twentieth centuries. He was an important spiritual counselor and ceremonial leader for his community, though he also converted to Christianity as an adult and was active as a catechist among his people. During this time, much of traditional religious life had gone underground, particularly when the United States government banned indigenous religious gatherings. People such as Black Elk walked in two worlds, simultaneously mastering two traditions, Christian and indigenous. In 1930, Black Elk worked with Neihardt to record part of his life story, in an effort toward preserving Lakota culture for future generations. Because he and other Lakota elders like him were able to negotiate two identities, cultural traditions of the Lakota survive to this day. Throughout his life he remained optimistic that Lakota culture would bloom once again, that the people would thrive, and that their spiritual and cultural strength would return. As he said to Neihardt at the conclusion of their interviews:

> At that time I could see that the hoop was broken and all scattered out and I thought, "I am going to try my best to get my people back into the hoop again." I am just telling you this, Mr. Neihardt. You know how I felt and what I really wanted to do is for us to make the tree bloom. On this tree we shall prosper ... we shall go back into the hoop and here we'll cooperate and stand as one ... our families will multiply and prosper after we get this tree to blooming.[18]

The Coast Salish: The Indian Shaker Church

Even before the first traders or missionaries reached the Pacific Northwest, Native culture there had been severely disrupted by the introduction of non-native diseases. Illnesses spread westward along Native trade routes from the east or were introduced during the brief stops made by Spanish, British, and American ships as they sailed along the Pacific coast. Smallpox epidemics occurred from 1800 to 1810, followed by tuberculosis in the 1820s, measles (brought by Hudson Bay traders) in 1821, and malaria in the 1830s. Between 1835 and 1847, local missionaries and traders reported outbreaks of meningitis, smallpox, influenza, mumps, and dysentery among the Native populations. With the arrival of traders and sailors also came syphilis and gonorrhoea. It has been estimated that Native populations in the Northwest dropped by 88% between 1805 and 1855.[19] Traditional healers sought to respond to these newly introduced diseases but found their methods inadequate. Coast Salish communities had been well equipped to respond to ailments that had been part of indigenous life for centuries, but the diseases brought by European invaders were completely new. When the first missionaries arrived in the Northwest, they found communities struggling with illness, and whose traditional economic, political, and social structures were dramatically disrupted. By the time treaties were made and reservations established in 1850, Native communities seemed on the brink of collapse.

Coast Salish communities seldom fought back against white encroachment with physical violence, but they did resist assimilation in other ways. They secured reservations throughout Washington State and, within those enclaves, sought to retain traditional spiritual practices. This was not easy, for Native religious practices were severely suppressed by Christian agents and missionaries from the Bureau of Indian Affairs. Spiritual leaders and those participating in winter ceremonials were threatened and imprisoned, and their rations withheld. Native people also sought to retain their right to traditional fishing, hunting, and gathering locations, and the spiritual and cultural traditions that accompanied these activities, but, as more and more Euroamerican settlers claimed more and more Coast Salish land, this became increasingly difficult. By the beginning of the twentieth century, many traditional Coast Salish fishing and shellfish gathering sites were lost, and the people were increasingly prevented from following their traditional subsistence patterns.

Among Coast Salish communities of British Columbia, the Canadian government undertook a concerted effort to wipe out one ceremonial expression in particular: the potlatch. This was an important gathering filled with ceremonial activity and characterized by the redistribution of wealth on an enormous scale. Social and spiritual status was secured within a potlatch through the distribution of food and valuables. But the potlatch also served an economic purpose. Individuals receiving gifts at a potlatch were obliged to return the favor. When agents and missionaries put an abrupt halt to the ceremony, assets were frozen, social and cultural hierarchies and rites of passage were disrupted, and an important ritual event was prevented. Whenever possible, winter ceremonials and potlatches moved underground, where they continued to be practiced regularly, although under a different guise and in less elaborate form.[20]

Amid such suppression of traditional religion, the **Indian Shaker Church** emerged, providing a means of maintaining core spiritual values, ethics, and approaches to wellness within a form and expression slightly more acceptable to the Christian authorities.[21] In 1882 the Squaxin Island Native John Slocum died, visited heaven, and spoke directly with Christ. He was told that he was to return to earth with a message for his people. They were to build a church and worship the Christian God, but to do so in a uniquely Indian way, using dream-inspired songs and prayers, spoken in their Native language. They were to lead moral lives, and give up smoking, alcohol, and gambling. In return, God would give them a new kind of medicine, one that cured every ailment. After three days in a death-like state, Slocum awoke, startling his family, and told them of his vision. The church was built, and Slocum began preaching to his people. A year later Slocum became very ill once more, and was again near death. His wife, Mary, was praying for him by a nearby creek, when she felt a spirit power come upon her. She began shaking all over and returned to the house, where she shook over her husband, praying and singing. By the next day, Slocum was completely recovered. This shake, Mary Slocum was certain, was the medicine that God had promised, and it quickly became the central feature of the movement.[22]

Restoring an individual to spiritual, physical, and emotional wholeness through the spirit power of Christ, was and is the primary focus of Shaker worship. Much of the Shaker Church is profoundly Christian: its members pray to God and Jesus, often meet in churches on Sundays and Wednesdays, and are called to worship by the ringing of church bells. They make the sign of the cross, pray for forgiveness and eternal salvation, sing hymns, and make frequent use of the number three, performing actions three times in a row. Scripture may also be referred to in the service, but many Shaker churches do not use the Bible. Many Shakers have argued that non-Native Christians need the Bible to hear from God, since they do not have direct access to Him through the experience of the Shake.[23]

The Indian Shaker Church was not merely a Christian impor-
tation; it also provided a means for maintaining a great deal of classical
Coast Salish spirituality. Severely suppressed by Indian Agents and
missionaries, traditional healers were some of the first to convert
to the Shaker Church, finding a space where they could continue
to sing, dance, heal, and lead their communities without risk of
persecution. The Shaker Church shared with traditional healers a
sense of disease causation: illness could be "shot" into one's body
by a malevolent person's spirit power, and illness could cause or be
caused by the loss of the soul, which could wander from the body.
If allowed to wander too far, the soul could not be recovered and
the patient might die. Healing occurred when a healer, empowered by
her or his (holy) spirit power or Shake, could draw the soul back to
the body, simultaneously removing whatever object had caused
the disease in the first place. Shaker healers, as described in H.G.
Barnett's seminal study in the early twentieth century,[24] would
draw the sickness out of the body, hold it in their hands, burn it in
flames, or place it in a jar to be buried outside the church, just as
traditional healers had done for centuries. Healing was brought about
not by the power of the individual but by the strength of the (holy)
spirit power working through the healer, another belief that was in
keeping with traditional spiritual practice. The ability to heal or be
healed was, as in indigenous religious practice, dependent on one's
relationship with that spirit. Shakers cultivated a relationship with
Christ, and they enacted that relationship through the Shake, much
as traditional Coast Salish healers had cultivated relationships with
spirit powers found in the natural world and honored them through
dances in the winter ceremonials.

Although the Shaker Church adopted a number of Christian
approaches to worship, most Indian Agents saw the services as having
far too much in common with traditional spirituality and still sought
to curtail Shaker meetings. Among the Skokomish, Squaxin Island,
and Nisqually tribes, for instance, Indian Agent Edwin Eells and his
brother, Presbyterian minister Myron Eells, vehemently opposed
the Shaker Church. Reverend Eells sought to prevent Shakers from
having access to the sick, and at times posted Presbyterian guards outside their homes. Shakers attempting to heal such patients were
imprisoned, put to forced labor, and publicly ridiculed. The meetings,

he argued, drew Indians away from Presbyterian services, providing an Indian alternative to the Euroamerican Church and, as such, disrupted the civilizing process of assimilating Native people into Euroamerican society.[25]

Despite such opposition (or perhaps inspired by it), church membership spread rapidly throughout the Northwest, and Shaker churches were established as far east as the Yakama Reservation in central Washington, north into British Columbia, and as far south as northern California. The Indian Shaker Church was often forced to practice covertly until 1910, when it was formally registered with the State of Washington as an official church, protected by the First Amendment. It continues today as a vitally important part of American Indian religious life throughout the Pacific Northwest, alongside longhouses and Christian churches. By incorporating Christian elements and adapting to Euroamerican bureaucratic systems, the Shaker Church provided a means through which the foundational principles of traditional spirituality could be preserved.

The Diné: The Long Walk

The Diné did not confront intensive missionary intervention until relatively late in the colonial period, although missionary efforts in the American Southwest began as early as 1598, when the Spanish explorer Juan de Oñate claimed the Pueblo communities for Spain. For the next century, while the Diné avoided almost any contact with Spanish missions, the Pueblo communities complied with Spanish authorities and tolerated Franciscan Fathers. The Franciscans constructed missions and soon began an aggressive conversion campaign. They differed markedly from their Jesuit colleagues in New France, who sought to work within Native culture and language as much as possible. The Franciscans fiercely opposed Pueblo religious and cultural life. As noted above, the decision to convert to Christianity often meant a Native person was cut off from his or her community and social network. This was particularly the case in Pueblo communities, where religious, social, and political lives were intricately interwoven. To turn to Christianity was essentially to lose one's place within one's family and society. Because of this, most Pueblo people resisted conversion. The Franciscans responded harshly, desecrating kivas (traditional ceremonial structures), destroying sacred objects and masks, and forbidding dances and meetings of sacred societies. They enforced attendance at daily Mass and punished the noncompliant with public beatings.[26]

Pueblo communities tolerated Spanish presence because the Spaniards had promised them God's protection from epidemic diseases and military protection from Apache and Diné raids. However, by 1670 disease was ravaging Pueblo communities, Apache and Diné raiding had increased dramatically, and the apparent failure of missionaries to honor their promises had led to a revival of traditional faith systems. The Franciscans responded by arresting sixty-seven Pueblo leaders, three of whom were executed. In 1680, led by the Pueblo spiritual leader Popé, the Pueblo communities revolted, driving the Spanish from the area, burning churches, and executing Franciscan friars, whom the Pueblo seemed particularly to blame for their suffering. By 1700, the Spanish had returned, and Pueblo communities allowed them a certain degree of political authority. However, from then on Franciscan missions would forever remain at the periphery of Pueblo society. The degree to which the Pueblo communities were able to keep Franciscan missionary efforts at bay would have consequences for the Diné as well.

The Diné had lived in the Four Corners regions of the Southwest for centuries before the arrival of the Spanish. Like the Apache, they spoke a dialect of the Athabascan language family and enjoyed a relatively nomadic lifestyle as hunter–gatherers. They coexisted with the Pueblo nations for most of this time, though a series of droughts in the seventeenth century and the lure of Spanish wealth and horses brought about an increase in raiding activities. It was the Pueblo revolt as well as their own nomadic life that protected the Diné from most missionary efforts until well into the eighteenth century. At that time, having acquired sheep and horses from the Spanish, the Diné took up a more sedentary lifestyle, cultivating cornfields, shepherding, and hunting. By the nineteenth century they were semi-nomadic, migrating seasonally between farming and herding, and enjoying a relatively wealthy, secure, and healthy lifestyle.

In the mid-nineteenth century, however, the Diné were confronted with a United States policy of confining all Native people onto reservations.

The Diné fiercely resisted these efforts to limit their landbase. Beginning in 1863, Kit Carson led a brutal campaign against the Diné. Unable to conquer them through sheer combat, he slaughtered Diné herds and destroyed crops and orchards. Within a year, a healthy population had been reduced to hunger and extreme disease. Faced with starvation, many people surrendered or journeyed farther west to escape. The people were exiled to the Bosque Redondo Reservation on a forced march, known as "The Long Walk," across 300 miles of desert, from Arizona to Fort Sumner, New Mexico. Within the first two weeks of the journey, 126 Diné died. At Bosque Redondo the army failed to supply proper shelter, sanitation, medical care, or food. Malnutrition and disease ran rampant. In the five years of this period of exile 25% of the Diné population perished of hunger, pneumonia, typhoid, dysentery, fevers, smallpox, measles, cholera, or the syphilis that was introduced by the U.S. army. In 1868, after intense negotiations and protests on the part of Diné leadership, the government finally recognized the disaster that Bosque Redondo had become, and the remaining 8,000 Diné returned to Arizona.[27]

After 1868, the Diné economy rebounded, as the communities concentrated on the annual cycle of shepherding and the cultivation of corn. Traditional Diné religion also flourished during this time, particularly in the form of healing ceremonies or chantways. Healing was and is the central focus of Diné spirituality, and Diné medicine men, or **hataałii**, worked to preserve the health and well-being of their people. This was particularly important, as disease rates were extremely high during this time, but doctors, clinics, hospitals, and tuberculosis sanitaria were notoriously underfunded, understaffed, and inadequate to Diné needs. From 1900, tuberculosis and trachoma ravaged the Diné reservation. By 1910, nearly a third of the population suffered from trachoma, and some government officials feared the entire reservation might eventually be threatened with blindness as a result. The worldwide influenza pandemic of 1918 also hit the reservation, killing nearly 10% of the Native population, and by the 1920s the tuberculosis death rate on the reservation was seventeen times that of the general population. By the 1950s the trachoma rate on the reservation was 1,163 times that of the general population, and the infant mortality rate was five times higher.[28]

Despite stiff opposition to traditional healers from Indian Agents and the concerted efforts of Euroamerican medical practitioners to lure Diné away from what they saw as a primitive mode of care, the Diné remained stubbornly committed to their traditional doctors. They avoided hospitals and clinics, seeing them as places tainted with death, filled with foreign and unsophisticated methods of curing, and run by people without cultural sensitivity or basic courtesy. Approaches to reservation health began to change in the 1930s, when John Collier first recommended that medical officials work with Diné *hataałii* rather than against or around them. Collier argued that the work of traditional medicine men was a necessary complement to Euroamerican medicine. In the 1950s, hospitals and clinics on the reservation began making overt gestures to include traditional healers, the use of the Diné language, and a cultural awareness that took into consideration Diné religious proscriptions against unnecessary body contact, the loss of bodily fluids or tissues, or contact with the dead.

Because of the Diné people's insistence on maintaining their own traditional healing practices despite vehement opposition from Euroamerican agents and missionaries, today a highly successful bi-cultural medical program exists on the Diné reservation. Doctors cooperate with *hataałii* and encourage their patients to make use of traditional healing in conjunction with Western medical care. Singers are able to perform chantways in or near hospitals, and medical staff continually work to be more culturally sensitive. In 1972, the Navajo Health Association was formed to encourage Diné to attend medical school, and many of the nurses and doctors on the reservation today are themselves Diné. In 1978, the Medicine Man's Association, later named the Dineh Spiritual and Cultural Society, was formed to preserve traditional knowledge and help to train future singers and healers.[29]

Conclusion

With the arrival of European settlers and missionaries, Native nations faced enormous challenges to their cultural and material survival. Epidemics and warfare destabilized indigenous cultures, facilitating white encroachment on Native lands and the introduction of new modes of subsistence, of social organization, and of spirituality. Throughout this history, Native people have been the focus of a variety of government policies aimed at assimilating their communities into Christianity and Euroamerican culture. Such policies were often driven (or at least accompanied) by a desire to free Native land for Euroamerican settlement. As the above histories demonstrate, assimilation efforts were never fully successful. Those that met with some success, such as John Collier's reforms, were those that sought to preserve indigenous culture, language, and traditions, while integrating certain useful aspects of Euroamerican religion or political life. The primary reason for cultural survival, however, is that Native peoples themselves largely refused aggressive assimilationist agendas, actively responding to such efforts with revitalizing religious movements, such as those led by Handsome Lake, Wovoka, and John and Mary Slocum. Such movements encouraged Native people to return to traditional ways of life and eschew the corrupting influences of white culture, while incorporating certain elements of Christianity that helped the people to survive. This can also be seen in the Diné experience, as they integrated traditional approaches to healing and spirituality alongside Euroamerican medicine, so as to meet the needs of their community while remaining adamant about their commitment to indigenous modes of healing and ceremony.

Chapter 1 of this book described three Native American religious gatherings: a Lakota Sun Dance, a Coast Salish First Salmon ceremony, and a Diné *Kinà`àldá*. This chapter places these ceremonial activities within the overall framework of twenty-first-century Lakota, Coast Salish, and Diné religion.

In the twenty-first century, indigenous spiritualities continue to thrive in all these communities, though their modes of expression have changed to meet new spiritual and material needs and new social and political contexts. One area in which this can be seen is in the formation of identity. Contemporary Native identity and spirituality draw not only from the specific tribal community, but also from a pan-tribal sensibility. Today, a Native person is Lakota, Coast Salish, or Diné, but also an American Indian. Having shared a common colonial history, tribes now share a common contemporary identity as a colonized people. For many, this may also mean participating in pan-tribal political and religious movements such as the American Indian Movement or the Native American Church.

The American Indian Movement: Contemporary political activism

Political and spiritual revival swept through what is sometimes referred to as Indian Country in the 1960s and '70s, inspiring both a reaffirmation of traditional spirituality and indigenous identity and a commitment to defending Native political rights. The American Indian Movement (AIM) first appeared on the political scene in 1969, when members of the group occupied Alcatraz Island in San Francisco Bay, a political demonstration that lasted nineteen months and caught the attention of national media.[1] AIM activists from San Francisco and Minneapolis joined together in their next major consciousness-raising effort, the Trail of Broken Treaties, an intertribal march on Washington D.C., protesting the government's failure to honor legally binding treaties such as the Fort Laramie Treaty. Officials at the Bureau of Indian Affairs (BIA) refused to speak with the protesters, who responded with a week-long occupation of the BIA office. Political activists received the most media attention, however, for an action they undertook in 1973: the occupation of Wounded Knee.

Wesley Bad Heart Bull, a Lakota, had been murdered by a white man; when his killer was tried for second-degree manslaughter and then acquitted by an all-white jury, members of AIM traveled to Custer, South Dakota, to protest the verdict. After the protest turned violent, AIM members left Custer and gathered at Wounded Knee to confer with traditionalist elders. The site of the infamous 1890 massacre was now a white-owned tourist attraction, complete with gift shop. The gathering of protesters became an occupation of the site, and AIM members, including traditionalist Lakota elders, were soon surrounded by tanks, laser-guided rifles, helicopters, and gunfire. The siege at Wounded Knee lasted seventy-one days. The event attracted enormous media coverage and support from Natives and non-Natives alike throughout the country. Two Native men were killed during the occupation: Buddy Lamont and Frank Clearwater. Thirteen additional people disappeared when packing in supplies for the protesters, and it has been assumed that they were killed as well.[2]

The Wounded Knee protest served as one of the most powerful symbols of emerging Native political activism in the late twentieth century, a movement that has since continued unabated. While it involved Native people from around the country, the event carried particular spiritual significance for the Lakota people, taking place as it did at the site of the 1890 massacre, and being led by traditionalist Lakota elders, with the support of younger traditionalist Native activists. Spirituality is a central feature of indigenous political activity today, just as it has been historically. AIM members sought out spiritual elders to guide their efforts and ensure that their actions were taken in the right way. Leonard Crow Dog, the spiritual leader of AIM, held a Ghost Dance during the Wounded Knee siege. It was

On February 27, 1973, members of the American Indian Movement, joined by Lakota traditionalists and elders, occupied the historic site of the 1890 Wounded Knee Massacre. For seventy-one days, while under fire from the FBI, the group dramatically protested federal incursions on tribal sovereignty and what they saw as an illegal and corrupt tribal government on the Pine Ridge reservation.

the first time since the 1890 massacre that a Ghost Dance had been held on Pine Ridge.

The political movements of the 1960s and '70s played an important role in Northwest Coast communities as well. When Coast Salish tribes signed treaties in the 1850s, they agreed to live on reservations and ceded large tracts of land for Euroamerican settlement. The treaties contained provisions that assured them the right to maintain a vital part of their traditional life: fishing. Traditional fishing practices had been carefully and ritually monitored to maintain the health and strength of fish runs year after year. Fish were harvested to meet local needs, and First Salmon ceremonies reminded the communities of the need to treat fish stocks with respect and care, always leaving enough to ensure a healthy harvest the next year. Nineteenth-century treaties promised "the right of taking fish at usual and accustomed grounds and stations."[3] Until the late nineteenth century, Euroamericans were dependent on trading with Native fisherman for salmon, thus assuring indigenous people a key role in emerging economies. However, the introduction of motorized boats in the early twentieth century enabled Euroamericans to catch increasing numbers of salmon and other fish themselves, and factories built in the late nineteenth and early twentieth centuries processed and canned enormous quantities of fish for shipment to far-off places. As Euroamerican commercial fishing in the Pacific Northwest grew, salmon runs dwindled, and Native people found themselves facing growing challenges to their subsistence fishing rights. By the 1930s, over-development and hydroelectric power threatened many salmon runs, flooding traditional indigenous fishing grounds, disrupting spawning patterns, and depriving the fish of cool, clear, running water, shaded streams, proper spawning grounds, and access to the ocean.

As runs decreased, state officials began regulating when, where, and how much fish could be caught at any given time. Native people, who caught only 2% of the overall salmon catch and who depended on the salmon as a primary food staple, were hit most severely by the new regulations. As runs declined, state laws made it increasingly difficult for Native people to catch in waters where they had fished for thousands of years. Given the central role of subsistence fishing and related ceremonies in Coast Salish spirituality, this posed a dire threat not only to Coast Salish food resources and physical well-being but also to the continuity of their cultural and spiritual traditions. As the twentieth century progressed, the rights to fish off reservation lands, guaranteed to Native people in their treaties, were increasingly being denied owing to Euroamerican over-consumption.

Despite harassment by local authorities, many Native people continued to fish traditional waters, protesting what they saw as violations of their treaty rights in what became known as fish-ins, held throughout the 1960s. Such political activism formed another part of the emerging American Indian Movement.[4] These widely publicized protests helped to raise awareness of contemporary Northwest Native communities and the role of salmon in their history and culture. The Boldt Decision of 1974 reestablished Native peoples' right to fish in traditional locations and their right to 50% of the annual salmon harvest at those locations. In the twenty-first century, the important role that salmon play in the spiritual and cultural economies of Coast Salish people has led many contemporary Coast Salish communities to take prominent roles both in the preservation and restoration of salmon habitat and in the opposition to the dams and over-fishing that threaten the survival of salmon populations. By the 1970s, Coast Salish nations along with other Northwest tribes were beginning to work with state and local agencies to protect salmon runs for future generations. It was during this time that First Salmon ceremonies, banned by the federal government from 1882 to 1934, were publicly revived. Today, a wide variety of indigenous grassroots efforts have joined with communities, environmental groups, and state agencies to devise creative ways of rescuing this vital part of the Northwest ecosystem.

The Native American Church

In the late twentieth century, pan-tribal political movements like the American Indian Movement became a part of contemporary life for many Native American people, for whom political concerns and spiritual activities were now coming together in a powerful way. Another growing pan-tribal movement that has come to have a prominent role in many people's lives is the Native American Church. The church has its origins in the use and veneration of peyote, a spineless cactus venerated and used in ceremonies by the Huichol Indians of northern Mexico for over 10,000 years. The Huichol consider the plant a gift from the creator, given to the Native people of North America for healing, prayer, and spiritual growth. The Huichol, along with the Carrizo, also of northern Mexico, taught the use of the sacrament peyote to the Lipan Apache in the early nineteenth century, and the Lipan, by the 1870s, had taught the tradition to the Kiowa, Plains Apache, and Comanche. From the 1880s to the 1920s, the practice spread widely throughout the Oklahoma tribes, and it was there that the contemporary form of the peyote ceremony took shape.

Quanah Parker (of the Comanche) was the most famous proponent of what eventually became the Native American Church, and taught his Half Moon style of worship to the Delaware, Caddo, Cheyenne, Arapaho, Ponca, Pawnee, and Osage nations. The Half

Moon style (so called because of a half-moon crescent of soil constructed at the altar inside the ceremonial tipi) has fewer Christian elements than the Big Moon (also known as Cross Fire) ceremony pioneered by John Wilson (of the Caddo). In 1914 the first peyote church, the First Born Church of Christ, was founded in Redrock, Oklahoma, and in 1918 the Native American Church was formally established with a membership of 12,000. This tradition offered Native people an alternative to Euroamerican Christianity at a time when many indigenous people had been deprived of their land, been settled on vastly reduced territories, and were suffering extreme levels of poverty, and political, cultural, and spiritual collapse. The peyote movement, like the Ghost Dance, provided a means of maintaining core indigenous values and traditions, gathering the community together in prayer to preserve its identity and culture, and doing so in a way that was distinctly Native.

Native American Church ceremonies are all-night prayer meetings in which participants partake of the sacred peyote, and sing and pray, accompanied by gourd rattles and water drums. Other important ritual elements include the use of tobacco, feather fans, a central fire and altar, reverence for the four cardinal directions, and, in the Big Moon style meetings, a Bible. During the service a Roadman, the ceremonial leader, holds a staff, sage, and a rattling gourd. He sings four songs and prays aloud, often in his Native language. Afterward, the staff, sage, and gourd are passed along to others in the circle, allowing everyone an opportunity to pray aloud. After this, the men and women attending the ceremony partake of the peyote, and then devote the remainder of the night to prayer, contemplation, and singing. In the morning, a woman who has been given the role of Dawn Woman brings water to the participants, a symbol of women's ability to bring new life. The group concludes with a hearty breakfast, after which everyone departs.[5]

By the early twentieth century, the peyote movement had spread beyond the Oklahoma territories, in part because it provided an alternative to Christian missionaries, and in part because it responded so well to the needs of American Indian people. Today the Native American Church has at least eighty chapters in seventy Native nations across the western half of the country. Estimates of its membership vary widely, from conservative estimates of 10,000 to generous estimates of 250,000. Members of the church find in meetings a powerful way to pray for their families and communities, and to seek healing and blessings for life transitions. The movement has been extremely successful, for example, in assisting many people to escape alcoholism and lead lives of sobriety.

Since the 1930s, the Native American Church has had a significant role on the Diné reservation in particular. The church was strongly opposed by Christian missionaries and also by traditionalist Diné, who saw the movement as a "new" religion threatening the survival of "classical" Diné spirituality. Seeking to protect their own religious traditions, the Diné tribal council at first sought to ban the church from the reservation, and church members were forced to conduct meetings in secret. However, by 1965 between 35% and 40% of Diné had participated in Native American Church meetings, and in 1967 the tribal council officially repealed the ban on church meetings on the reservation. It has recently been estimated that at least half of the Diné on the reservation have participated in Native American Church meetings, and most of these also participate in traditional Diné chantways. With perhaps 60,000 participants, the Diné make up the largest tribal group within the Native American Church. Meetings are held in the Diné language, and have been modified to reflect Diné philosophy.[6] The goal of Diné Native American Church meetings is to cultivate *Sa'a Naaghai Bik'eh Hozho*: balance, long life, wisdom. Among the Diné, the Native American Church has provided another means of maintaining traditional Diné philosophical principles and ethics, and has done so in a way that is distinctly indigenous.[7]

Contemporary Lakota spirituality: Situating the Sun Dance

Chapter 1 described one instance of a Lakota Sun Dance (*wiwanyang wacipi*), a tradition marked by personal sacrifice, prayer, and reverence for the sun and the four directions. The other central ceremonies brought to the Lakota by White Buffalo Calf Woman include *Inipi* or *Inikagapi* ("to make or renew life force"), *Haŋbleceyapi* ("crying for a vision," the vision quest), **Hunkapi lowanpi** ("they sing over those over whom the *Hunka* [chosen] staffs are held"), **Isnati Awicalowan** ("when she lives alone, they sing over her"), **Wanagi**

Yuhapi ("they keep the ghost"), and ***Tapa Wankeyeyapi*** ("throwing a ball"). Such ceremonies are generally conducted by a medicine man or woman. In the Lakota tradition, these figures are given the gift of leadership because they have acquired powerful spiritual assistance through prayer, fasting, and vision seeking. Those who have been given visions are assisted by powerful spirit helpers who guide them throughout their lives. All of these ceremonies, while they follow a common pattern, are open to the inspired variation of individual holy men and women. Their visions and spirit powers may direct them to conduct a ceremony in a particular mode, incorporating various symbols or rituals. Individuals chosen for spiritual leadership undergo a lifetime of spiritual training, guided by other elders, who assist in the interpretation of dreams and visions and the enactment of various rituals and ceremonies.[8]

According to Martin Brokenleg, Lakota ceremonies share a basic structure. Each begins with preparation and invitation. During this time, participants prepare themselves physically and spiritually for the ritual. In the second stage, individuals participating in the ceremony receive instruction from elders as to how they are to proceed and how they are to make sense of their experience. The next stage of the ceremony centers on a particular set of symbols, typically accompanied by prayers, song, or ritual activities. Finally, ceremonies are concluded, and a feast is given to thank those who have assisted in the process and to honor the elders who have led the ceremony.[9]

One of the most important Lakota ceremonies, *Inipi* or *Inikagapi*, has this essential structure.[10] As mentioned in Chapter 2, the sweat lodge is a central aspect of traditional and contemporary Lakota religious practice. Participants enter the domed structure and are seated around a central pit filled with heated stones. This setting mirrors the Lakota myth of creation, where the circular cosmos, at the beginning, consisted of nothing but stone. As water is poured on the rocks, the spirit of the stones is released in the form of steam. The heat and darkness provide a place for physical and spiritual cleansing, for introspection, and for prayer. Each person in the lodge has an opportunity to pray, moving clockwise in a circle. A sweat lodge ceremony will typically be conducted for four rounds, interrupted in the third round for prayers offered with a sacred pipe. The *Inipi* plays an important role in many other Lakota religious activities.

The Sun Dance and other religious efforts are often preceded and then followed by a sweat.

A second major ceremony was also discussed briefly in Chapter 2: *Haŋbleceyapi*, the process by which one prepares for and seeks out a vision. Today, both men and women freely participate in this activity, although many debate the degree to which gender defined one's participation in the past. Today, regardless of gender, when someone seeks a vision, he or she first seeks out a spiritual elder to guide them through the process. They begin with a sweat, to purify the vision seeker. Elders then lead him or her to a secluded place, and prepare the vision space by marking off the four directions and encircling the area with tobacco ties. Tobacco ties are made of square pieces of cloth, filled with a pinch of tobacco and tied with a string. Each tie is made with a prayer. An altar may be placed in the enclosure, but then the participant is left alone without food or water or other distractions for up to four days. The ceremony is concluded with another sweat, during which the initiate will share the experience with spiritual elders, and they will help to interpret any dreams and visions.

A third ceremony still practiced by contemporary Lakota is a rite of adoption, referred to as *Hunkapi Iowanpi.* In this ceremony, new kinship relations are established. This ceremony is not just for adopting children but for establishing any kind of familial bond. It was historically a central ceremonial mode in which the Lakota established kinship relationships with other nations and divisions; it thus acted as a way to keep the peace between communities. Kinship and obligations to one's extended relations are central to Lakota culture, and hence this ceremony is an extremely important one. All ceremonies are conducted with the intention of meeting the needs of one's community and of working to honor one's responsibilities and obligations to one's kin. In this one, such relationships are ritually solidified. There are variations within it, but in some traditions the individual is sung over, with a pipe stem waved over them. A new name is given to them, and they are fed with cherry juice and dried meat.

Another very important ceremony brought by White Buffalo Calf Woman is *Isnati Awicalowan*, the coming-of-age ceremony for young Lakota women. At her first menstruation, a young woman remains in seclusion for four days. During this time she is taught by older women about women's skills and responsibilities, including cooking, weaving, basketry, sewing, and beading. The girl's sponsor, often her grandmother, takes on the role of White Buffalo Calf Woman, instructing the girl in morality and the Lakota spiritual way of life. At the conclusion of the ceremony, the girl has been transformed into a woman. Her family honors this new identity through a feast and giveaway, declaring her status as a valued and respected member of their family.[11]

Wanagi Yuhapi is a mourning ceremony, intended to facilitate grieving over a lost family member. With the guidance of spiritual elders, parents or other family members who are unable to release their emotional tie to a deceased loved one will cut a lock of hair from the top of the person's head. The lock of hair is considered to hold the person's spirit and is placed in a special container, kept in a special place, and spoken to and cared for throughout the next year. During this year, family members must honor certain ritual restrictions. Their behavior must be carefully controlled; their speech and mode of dress must also adhere to strict guidelines. The family should be careful to honor the good works of their deceased relative, continuing that person's efforts. Finally, at the end of the year, mourning songs and prayers are sung, and farewells are said. The lock of hair is burned, and then the memory of the deceased is honored through a feast and giveaway.

Tapa Wankeyeyapi is a highly stylized game, intended to work as both a ceremony and a pedagogical tool. The ball used in the game was traditionally made from buffalo hide, and decorated with symbols. As with all ceremonies, an elder leads the event, preparing the space by praying with a ceremonial pipe and constructing an altar. A young woman stands as representative of the people and tosses the ball in the four directions, reminding the people of their dependence on both the land and the bison, and recalling the way in which White Buffalo Calf Woman rolled to the four directions, becoming a white bison, a yellow bison, a red bison, and a black bison. Finally, the Sun Dance, the seventh ceremony brought by White Buffalo Calf Woman and described at length in Chapter 1, is a celebration of sacrifice for the well-being of the community, and a commitment to prayer.

These seven ceremonies are only some of the most common rites practiced by contemporary Lakota people. Other traditions upheld by contemporary Lakota include ceremonies focusing on healing, spirit calling, name giving, honoring, giving thanks, and offering blessings. In fact, very few important activities are carried out without some prayer and a sense of its spiritual meaning. One of the most common groups of individual and collective spiritual activities is that comprising the various pipe ceremonies. White Buffalo Calf Woman gave the people a pipe, and instructed them in the ways of praying with it, offering smoke and prayers to the four directions. Other sacred pipes are held by various families and medicine men and are at times kept alongside sacred bundles, opened only at times of ritual and prayer. While some particular pipes are particularly well known, any Lakota individual may also own a sacred pipe, using it in private prayer and ceremony. In a pipe ceremony, the pipe is carefully unwrapped, assembled, and held aloft to the four directions while prayers and songs are offered. Often the pipe is then passed around the circle of collected people, so that all those assembled may pray with the pipe before passing it on to others.[12]

Such traditional ceremonies are often practiced alongside Christian traditions: many Lakota are Episcopalian or Catholic, but they tend to be highly ecumenical, prioritizing their unity as Lakota over division of denomination. Since the 1960s, Christian leaders on the reservations have become increasingly open to incorporating elements of traditional indigenous spirituality into their Christian worship. Many Lakota see no contradiction between participating in a sweat lodge, vision quest, or Sun Dance and being a devout Christian, although some have left Christian practice to engage in their traditional beliefs. Rituals and symbols are interpreted in ways that allow for the integration of the Christian message, as well as key Lakota notions such as a reverence for one's ancestors and the earth. Some Lakota people are also active members of the Native American Church, incorporating the use of the sacrament peyote within all-night prayer meetings. The Native American Church is intentionally open in its theology, allowing individual members to interpret the symbols and prayers of the ceremony in ways that mesh with their own individual indigenous traditions and their Christian faith, stressing unity of practice over consistency of belief.

Coast Salish longhouse spirit dancing

Previous chapters have already discussed the important role of the potlatch, First Salmon ceremonies, and the Indian Shaker Church in Coast Salish religious life. Despite attempts to limit their practice, potlatches remain an enormous part of contemporary Native life in the Northwest, functioning as ceremonial means of celebrating rites of passage, conveying honor and gratitude, and passing on ritual objects or rank; First Salmon ceremonies have become common once again in recent years; and the Indian Shaker Church is an active participant in much of Coast Salish spirituality. Very often, an individual is a member either of a Christian church, or of the Indian Shaker Church, or of a traditional longhouse. However, some individuals participate in all of these, moving from one tradition to another at different times in their lives.[13] This section focuses on Coast Salish longhouse traditions, in particular spirit dancing.

Longhouse (or smokehouse) traditions enjoyed a remarkable renaissance among the Coast Salish in the late twentieth century. In the 1970s, anthropologist Pamela Amoss was amazed at the rising numbers of dancers she witnessed.[14] In the 1990s, anthropologist Crisca Bierwert again studied Coast Salish longhouse spirit dancing, and observed that dancing had actually increased exponentially since Amoss recorded her observations.[15]

According to Amoss, spirit dancing is referred to in some Coast Salish communities as syó'wən, a term used to refer both to the actual spirit dance itself and to the guardian spirit that the dance is meant to honor. As previously mentioned, such activities are xœ'xœ, a dangerous, powerful means of connecting the supernatural with the natural world. Spirit dancing takes place in a longhouse, generally during the wintertime. A dance comprises three important activities: hospitality, when guests are thanked for coming and are fed; the spirit dance itself, in which dancers, singers, and drummers all participate; and a period of "work," when speeches are made, witnesses are called upon, and gifts are distributed.[16]

Guardian spirits, as discussed in Chapter 2, are centrally important to traditional Coast Salish spirituality. In the contemporary era, it is very rare that someone might venture out on an isolated vision quest in search of a guardian spirit, but such spirits still make themselves known, typically approaching individuals during times of emotional crises, such as illness or grieving the loss of a loved one. Spirits can also be inherited within a family and passed along through generations. When someone has been chosen by a spirit, that person may become sick, suffering from spirit sickness until he or she is initiated at a winter spirit dance. Guardian spirits give an individual a spirit song and dance, which the individual must then perform at a winter dance.

Amoss and Bierwert, both of whom worked closely with Coast Salish elders and with Coast Salish cultural expert Vi Taqwšəblu Hilbert, provide careful descriptions of winter spirit dances in their work. As they emphasize, initiation at winter dances involves the support and guidance of spiritual elders, who work with initiates, helping them to sing their song. To honor their syó'wən properly, initiates should dance, care for their dance regalia, abstain from alcohol, and regularly bathe in a river. Unlike northern coastal tribes, which use elaborate carved masks within their ceremonial dancing, most Coast Salish spirit dancers do not wear masks, though initiates may wear braided strands of wool, cedar, or raffia hanging down over their face and eyes. Each dancer, as he or she is moved by their syó'wən to sing and dance, will be guided around the room by attendants, to ensure that he or she does not trip, fall, or bump into any other participants. Each dancer has his or her own unique dance and song, though they also follow a set pattern of performance. Each dancer will complete a full circuit of the room, circling as many as three times before being guided back to his or her seat by helpers and attendants.

The success of spirit dancing in the contemporary era is due in part to the degree to which it so successfully meets the needs of twenty-first-century Coast Salish people. Dances provide a means of curing physical, spiritual, and emotional illness. An individual suffering from depression, addiction, fatigue, or any number of other ailments may find spiritual strength through initiation and dancing. According to Coast Salish tradition, diseases are often caused by the loss of an individual's soul, which has strayed too far from their body. Through dancing, the individual can receive strength and healing, and a return to wholeness.

According to Amoss, syó'wən also meets other vitally important social needs in addition to healing. Spirit dancing binds the community more closely together. In large part, this is simply because of the enormous amount of effort and material resources needed to put on a dance. The longhouse must be kept up, food must be provided for everyone that attends, wood provided for heat, and so on. Dancing provides a place for the community to confer rank and honor on worthy individuals, as most dances are followed by a giveaway, a contemporary gift-giving ceremony similar to a potlatch. It is here that honor is bestowed, names given, and ritual responsibilities handed down to the next generation. These activities provide a space for the redistribution of property, for sharing, and for supporting each other through lean times. Public loans may also be distributed at this time, as individuals exchange money to help elders and needy families.

The Indian Shaker Church is another important part of religious life for many Salish people in the Northwest. It draws on the same indigenous heritage as the syó'wən, to provide a means for spiritual empowerment. Shakers also focus on curing within their ceremonies, and on retrieving lost souls. However, the Shaker Church differs from syó'wən in its ties to Christianity and its incorporation of Christian modes of prayer, ritual, symbol, and church structure.

In addition to observing longhouse traditions and their involvement with the Shaker Church, many Coast Salish people are also members of Methodist, Catholic, or Pentecostal churches. Pentecostalism in particular enjoyed an increase in membership before the 1970s, but participation began to wane with the revitalization of spirit dancing.[17] It is interesting to note that three of the most popular modes of spiritual practice among the Coast Salish all emphasize similar things. Syó'wən, Pentecostalism, and the Indian Shaker Church all allow for a direct communion with a spiritual being, and provide a focus on healing. What the Shaker and longhouse traditions provide that Pentecostalism does not are traditions uniquely grounded in indigenous practice and spirituality, expressions that affirm one's identity as a Northwest Coast Native.

Diné chantways and sand paintings

Like that of the Coast Salish, contemporary Diné religious life is largely split between three traditions: Christianity (particularly Pentecostalism),

ART FOCUS

Diné sand painting

DINÉ SAND PAINTING is a dry technique using colored sands and ground minerals, which are slowly trickled from between the thumb and forefinger onto a smooth patch of sand. Materials are meticulously gathered from the surrounding landscape, from multicolored sandstone and other mineral resources, then brought back to the *hooghan*, where they are carefully ground between rocks and sieved through a cloth to a fine, smooth texture. Red, yellow, and white powders are made from ground sandstone, black is derived from charcoal, and a gray-blue is acquired by mixing black and white.

Sand paintings can range in size from 12 inches to 12 feet in diameter, depending on the type of chantway being performed. Their function is to prepare the ceremonial *hooghan* for the arrival of the *ye'ii*, or Holy People, who will be welcomed into the ritual space. Each sand painting represents a microcosm of the Diné cosmos, including the four directions; the colors associated with the four directions (white, blue, yellow, black); the four sacred mountains; minerals; Holy People; and types of corn and other plants associated with each of the four directions. Other symbols may include animals or other Holy People associated with the myth of the chantway, messenger winds, and protective rainbows. These are not merely symbolic representations but also participate in the reality and spirit of those things that they represent.

A Diné spiritual leader directs the making of a sand painting, although assistants will often do most of the actual creation. The spiritual practitioner prepares the space, covering the water-filled bowl with *kétłoh* powder (a mixture of dry plant materials) and charcoal. His or her assistants then begin the sand painting itself. The painting is oriented toward the east, the direction of dawn, birth, and new beginnings. A guardian spirit, often in the image of a rainbow, surrounds the other three sides. The assistants work diligently for what may be hours, while the ceremonial leader carefully observes to make sure that no elements are left out or done inappropriately. When the sand painting is done, thirteen prayersticks are stood in the sand surrounding the painting. The end result is a safe space, where the patient is surrounded by beauty.

Each chantway is based on a sacred story, and the sand painting represents pivotal moments of that story. The hero or heroine of these sacred stories undertook a great journey, and through that journey was transformed, healed, made new. Through sand paintings, patients are able to renew their relationship with the Holy People and the four directions.

The sand paintings used in chantways were gifts to the Diné from the Holy People. When they are completed in the context of a ceremonial application they are sacred. For instance, in the Coyoteway chantway the sand paintings were not deemed sacred until prayersticks were added, and until corn pollen and cornmeal were sprinkled. Some Diné practitioners, after negotiations with scholars, have agreed to have some of the designs photographed to be published in books of learning. Commercially available sand paintings by Diné artists are only partial representations of some of the images found within sand paintings, and not recreations of ceremonial works. Such images have become a respected art form for many contemporary Diné.

A sand painting is created on the floor of a hooghan, *the traditional Diné house.*

the Native American Church, and traditional Diné ceremony. Native American Church ceremonies, described above, appeal to many Diné for a variety of reasons. Like the Indian Shaker Church, the Native American Church is a distinctly indigenous mode of spiritual expression, but one that also allows for the incorporation of various Christian themes and symbols. Also like the Indian Shaker Church, the Native American Church is a space wherein one can acknowledge a pan-tribal Indian identity. In a service or meeting such as this, one is not just Lakota, Nisqually, or Diné—one is a Native American and shares in that broader identity and experience. However, within tribally specific religious traditions such as those that take place in the longhouse or, for the Diné, in the *hooghan*, the individual takes part in rituals, ceremonies, and storytelling that link him or her directly to his or her own tribal community and nation, to their own indigenous landscape, and to their own family lineage. Hence, tribally specific traditions can offer many things that pan-tribal movements or Christianity cannot.

For the Diné, traditional spirituality is centered on an elaborate tradition of ceremonial chantways, each of which is geared toward a particular type of healing. Individuals consult with specialized diagnosticians who have the ability to discern which ceremony or chantway is appropriate for which individual. Each of the chantways is intended to cure individuals of physical, mental, emotional, or spiritual maladies. Some are intended as preventative medicine, to bless someone who is going out into the world to attend school, to join the military, or to undertake a long journey. Other chantways are used to integrate back into the community someone who has returned from such an arduous undertaking. To be a ceremonial leader, or *hataałii*, an individual is apprenticed to an experienced elder, who will teach him or her the prayers, songs, sand paintings, herbal medicines, philosophy, history, stories, and other ritual practices necessary to enact these chantways. Because of the enormous amount of ritual and liturgical knowledge that an individual must acquire, such apprenticeships commonly take most of a lifetime.

Chantways last from one to nine days and typically comprise a series of prayers, songs, sand paintings, blessings, and ritual sweat baths. One central group of song chantways is that of the Blessingway chantways, which are intended to grant blessings to the individual and to protect them against future harm, rather than cure them of present ailments. During Blessingway chants a ceremonial basket or *ts'aa'* is used. The Diné emergence narrative is woven into the symbolic designs on the basket, which is used to remind the individual of her or his place within the Diné cosmology.[18]

Enemyway, Evilway, and Lifeway chants are also intended to prevent a patient from coming to harm. Enemyway chants are performed after an individual has returned from a dangerous place such as war or a burial. Likewise, Evilway and Lifeway chants divert evil influences and set the patient on a good path.

The largest group of chantways is intended to cure illness; and is referred to as the Holyway group. There are over sixty different types of Holyway chants, divided into categories such as Windway, Beadway, Eagleway, Big Star Way, Flintway, Mountainway, Hailway, Nightway, Shootingway, Waterway, Chircauhua Windway, and Beautyway.[19] Holyway ceremonies commonly last for five nights. The *hataałii* will sing the chantway, conducting a series of ceremonies and rituals throughout the night. Typically, the ritual activity of the five nights can be broken into two parts—the first part purifying the patient and sending away evil influences, and the second part welcoming wholeness, goodness, and strength into the patient. Each chantway has a unique series of songs, prayers, and rituals, all of which must be performed perfectly. Each Holyway chant is founded on an origin story. These stories describe the journey of a hero, who traveled to the spirit world, secured ritual knowledge, medicines, and other blessings such as corn or tobacco, and brought them back to her or his people. Throughout the five nights, the patient is led through songs and prayers that enable her or him to associate her- or himself fully with this hero's journey.

The patient is carefully taken through the ceremonial process, identifying every part of his or her body and self with the bodies of the Holy People, as they are directed in prayer and meditation by the singer. One way in which this is accomplished is through dry sand paintings, created on the *hooghan* floor.[20] These represent images and symbols from the hero's story, the four directions, and other geographical features within the Diné sacred geography. Over 1,200 different sand paintings are used in fifty-six different Holyway chants. Each one is both a visual representation of the origin story of the chantway and a literal manifestation of the beings and powers inherent in that story. The hero of the chantway's story received the design for the sand painting and brought it back to her or his people. Hence, such designs are considered sacred, and they are viewed as temporary copies of permanent paintings kept by the Holy People in the spirit world. Sand paintings are made of ground rock and other minerals, painstakingly crushed by hand with a mortar and pestle. A *hataałii* and his or her assistants make the paintings themselves. The sand paintings must be made perfectly in order to be efficacious: if they are made inaccurately or mistreated in any way, dire consequences and illnesses can result. Because these images are so sacred, they are newly made and destroyed each time they are needed, to prevent them from being misused or stolen. Sand paintings are referred to in Diné as *'iikááh*, a word that translates as "the place where the gods come and go." The term is illustrative of the role that sand paintings have in ceremonial chantways. They are considered to be extremely porous spaces through which the spiritual power of the Holy People, the *yé'ii*, is able to pass.

Dry sand paintings function as temporary altars, inviting the Holy People to join the ceremony. Common images include plants such as corn, beans, squash, and tobacco, rain clouds, and the four sacred mountains of the four directions, as well as the Holy People themselves, often situated in the four directions, generally in male–female pairs. Commonly a guardian, often a rainbow, surrounds and protects the sand painting, which is open to the east, where, protecting this entrance, is a pair of guardian figures. Paintings can range from one foot to twelve feet in diameter, and can take as long as ten hours to complete. Sand paintings are made freehand and take incredible skill and patience. When the painting is complete, the image is blessed with pollen and sung over with songs from the chantway.[21]

The patient is seated on the painting, facing east, and the *hataałii* works to identify the patient with the Holy People in the painting, singing over the patient and touching parts of the painting, followed by the corresponding parts of the patient's body. He may do this four times, accompanied by various other ritual activities. The patient is, in this way, placed within the story through song, prayer, and ritual. According to some interpretations, sand paintings are considered to be spiritual doorways, sacred spaces through which goodness and wholeness are drawn from the Holy People to the patient, and sickness and evil are drawn from the patient into the sand painting. After the ceremony, the painting is destroyed and taken to the north of the *hooghan*, where the elements, now filled with the patient's sickness, are returned to the earth. In other interpretations, sand paintings act as physical manifestations of the *ye'ii*, images through which the Holy People are called, welcomed, and invoked. Through sand paintings and chantways, the patient is restored to a proper relationship with the Holy People, correcting an imbalance within that relationship and hence restoring the patient to health.

Sand paintings also work effectively to locate the patient within a sacred story, allowing a means for the individual to experience a tangible exchange with the Holy People and a transformation of the self. Another way this transformation is accomplished is through prayer. The patient will repeat the words of the prayers in the first person present, placing him or herself within the story. For instance: "Now I am walking through the sacred fields. Now my body is being made new. Now my feet are made new. Now my soul is made new. Now I am walking in beauty."[22] The singer will guide the patient through this process, identifying each part of the patient's body with the hero and the Holy People:

> Put your feet down with pollen.
> Put your hands down with pollen.
> Put your head down with pollen.
> Then your feet are pollen;
> Your hands are pollen;
> Your body is pollen;
> Your mind is pollen;
> Your voice is pollen;
> The trail is beautiful.
> Be still.[23]

Diné chantways serve important social as well as spiritual functions. A patient depends on her or his extended family, clan, and community for a chantway to take place. The family must find a traditional *hooghan* to house the ceremony, and the services of a *hataałii* must be secured. Dozens or even hundreds of people may attend a chantway to convey their support and prayers for the patient.

Everyone who attends must be welcomed and fed, an endeavor that can be extremely expensive and labor-intensive. Additionally, gifts are distributed following a gathering to all those who contributed their time and effort. Hence, such ceremonies are extremely time-consuming and costly. Because of this, chantways draw people together, pooling their resources and demonstrating their support for the patient. Kinship networks are strengthened, the importance of community is reinforced, and the patient in particular is shown how valued she or he is within the extended family and community.

Conclusion

Religious life for contemporary Native American people is a complex negotiation of traditions. Christian churches exist alongside traditional indigenous religious practices. Indigenous religious movements such as the Native American Church and the Indian Shaker Church successfully fuse indigenous practice and Christian symbols in a way that meets many people's contemporary spiritual and cultural needs. What should be clear is that there is no single way in which contemporary Native people practice their faith and traditions. They have crafted modes of religious expression that are directly meaningful and relevant to their lives, both politically and spiritually. Some have chosen to convert wholeheartedly to Christianity and maintain an active and vibrant faith life in these churches. Others have joined traditions that integrate elements of Christianity and traditional spirituality, while still others have maintained classical indigenous traditions, working alongside spiritual elders in their own communities to maintain and revive these practices. Considering the history of colonialism and evangelization discussed in Chapter 3, the degree to which indigenous religious practices are still flourishing today is remarkable. In the twenty-first century, traditional Lakota rituals and ceremonies, spirit dancing in Coast Salish longhouses, and Diné chantways in traditional *hooghans* are still being practiced and celebrated, and are still a vital part of many people's lives.

The previous four chapters have presented a brief overview of Native American religious practices and the historical events that have helped to shape them. This chapter presents some key issues that are shaping the future of traditional religious life in the twenty-first century. As earlier chapters have demonstrated, Native cultures and beliefs have survived centuries of challenges. They have done so through creativity and adaptation, modifying practices to meet the changing needs of Native people, incorporating elements of Euroamerican culture but maintaining the core principles and practices of traditional spirituality. This process of cultural transformation was certainly not limited to the colonial period, for, as was discussed in Chapter 1, Native traditions and cultures have always responded to ecological, economical, and social transitions. Although Native cultures have demonstrated that they are here to stay, in the twenty-first century they face continued  challenges to both their cultural and their ecological survival. Key areas of concern such as intellectual property rights, repatriation, sovereignty, the protection of sacred sites, and the preservation of endangered ecosystems are certain to be central in guiding the direction of indigenous religious life in the coming decades. These issues are discussed here as two distinct but interconnected concerns: cultural survival and ecological survival.

Cultural survival: New Age appropriation, intellectual property rights, repatriation, and sovereignty

Native American religious life in the twenty-first century faces a number of threats. One of the most ironic of contemporary challenges to Native spirituality is its popularity, which has resulted in its commodification in the New Age marketplace. In the late twentieth and early twenty-first centuries, Native American religious practices have become a desirable commodity, marketable through a variety of books, music, and weekend retreats that claim to offer Euroamericans access to the religious practices and spiritual beliefs of Native people. Unfortunately, many of these materials are distortions of traditional beliefs or even outright fabrications, and many of the authors write without proper instruction, initiation, or permission from the people from whom they profit. Many Native communities have expressed deep concern over this trend. As described in Chapter 3, from the mid-nineteenth to the mid-twentieth centuries, Native traditions were essentially outlawed, and the federal government, guided by assimilationist ideals, actively sought to suppress such practices. Such suppression, at times violent, was deeply unsettling. For some Native activists and scholars, the New Age commodification of these traditions today fits within this history of theft and colonization.[1]

It may seem strange that a spiritual movement purporting to revere Native traditions should be seen by most traditional Native people as profoundly offensive. Many contemporary Native social critics, however, argue that the history of colonization has been a series of thefts: of land, of resources, of life. To them, the contemporary appropriation of Native traditions by New Age authors and gurus is simply the most recent theft. As Margo Thunderbird wrote in 1988:

> They came for our land, for what grew or could be grown from it, for the resources in it and for our clean air and pure water. They stole these things from us, and in the taking, they also stole our free ways and the best of our leaders, killed in battle or assassinated. And now, after all that, they've come for the very last of our possessions; now they want our pride, our history, our spiritual traditions. They want to rewrite and remake these things to claim them for themselves."[2]

Advocates of New Age literature and spirituality argue that each individual should be free to pursue whatever religious tradition he or she feels drawn to, regardless of ethnicity or cultural origin, and that excluding non-Native people from Native spirituality is racist and exclusivist. Native authors have responded with several critiques of the New Age approach. First, they argue that such an approach takes indigenous traditions out of their cultural context, frequently merging Native cultures without regard for their distinct traditions, languages, and histories. These practices distort the meaning and significance of religious practices, because indigenous spirituality is inseparable from the broader cultural context. Religion cannot thus be seen in isolation from kinship structures, subsistence activities, landscape, history, and identity. Further, New Age appropriation implies a continuation of the colonizing process, a process of taking from Native communities all that they have to offer, without demonstrating a genuine commitment to those communities, their sovereignty, or their sustainability.

Native critics also argue that New Age approaches show little respect for the tradition itself. Indigenous religious traditions, as have been described in this book, are passed down through lifetimes of careful study and apprenticeship. To lead such ceremonies or rituals requires years, or even decades, of learning and participation in community life. In many cases, only certain individuals within a particular Native community, perhaps only those who have been initiated into a particular sacred society, have access to certain types of knowledge.

Traditional Native American perspectives on knowledge itself differ profoundly from Euroamerican views. While Euroamerican culture is largely dominated by an ideal of scientific inquiry and a widespread belief in one's "right to know," indigenous cultures typically see knowledge as demanding responsibility. Knowledge keepers have responsibility to use their wisdom appropriately, and they also have a responsibility to restrict that knowledge from individuals for whom it would not be suitable. Certain types of knowledge are best withheld from some, particularly those who are not prepared or not able to understand what is being presented to them. Most Native American religious practices are seen not as philosophies but, rather, as means of interacting with extremely powerful and dangerous spiritual beings. Native people have argued that individuals who truly believed in the spiritual powers behind the traditions would not approach them in such a cavalier fashion.

Most important, as many Native authors have explained, is the issue of respect. Spiritual traditions, beliefs, and practices belong to the communities from whom they come. Native communities want to

ART FOCUS

Contemporary Coast Salish art

CONTEMPORARY ARTISTS on the Northwest Coast have become known throughout the world for their unique styles of carving, printing, and painting, invoking images that are both abstract and representative of human and animal form. While the traditions of the Northern Coast such as the Kwakiutl (Kwak'waka'wakw), the Tlingit, and Haida tend to be better known, Coast Salish communities have long had a powerful artistic tradition of their own. The Coast Salish artistic tradition of today is both traditional and contemporary, invoking images representative of Northwest oral traditions, clans, and spirit powers, often using modern media.

Spiritual themes are prevalent throughout much of Coast Salish artwork. In particular, the viewer can note representations of transformation, in which human and animal forms continually merge and shift into one another. Such images evoke the oral traditions of Transformer, who set the world in order at a time when every living creature in the world was a person, having not yet been divided into their separate forms and species. The sense that, internally, all sentient beings share the same personhood can be seen within these morphing images, as salmon becomes man, and man becomes salmon.

The presence of spirit powers can also be seen, as animal figures are present alongside, within, or on top of a human form, empowering it with speech and ability. This may be discerned in a transformation mask, in which an individual wears the image of a bear, which is both human and bear simultaneously. This shared identity built through reciprocal relationships is a foundational principle of Coast Salish spirituality, played out in contemporary artwork in innumerable ways.

Family and clan histories can also be discerned in these images. Coast Salish oral traditions often link the origin of a family or clan to an ancient intermarriage with another species—bear people, salmon people, or thunder people—and such family origins are certainly discernible in some of these works. Family crests can be expressed within this pervasive theme of transformation, where human people and animal people are able to negotiate these relationships through artistic expression.

Among the many Coast Salish artists working today is Susan Point, who has lived her entire life on the Musqueam First Nation Reservation in Vancouver, B.C. She draws from traditional Coast Salish themes, particularly traditional Coast Salish spindle whorls. She began carving such spindle whorls, and went on to create silkscreen prints, experimenting with Coast Salish designs and style. Her work steps outside of traditional techniques, using foil embossing, paper casting, linocut printing, and lithography, and incorporating such media as glass, concrete, polymer, stainless steel, and cast iron. Despite the contemporary mode of expression, her work maintains a loyalty to Coast Salish traditional style and symbol, highlighting the themes of spiritual transformation and the interrelationship between the human and the more-than-human worlds. Her print *Reflection of the Sockeye People* is a powerful representation of traditional Coast Salish spirituality in a contemporary context. The spirit of salmon people, honored through First Salmon ceremonies, is here depicted in free-flowing form.

Susan Point, Reflection of the Sockeye People, *1990. Serigraph, 15¹⁄₂ × 17 ins.*

control how their religious traditions are practiced and promulgated. Their spiritual leaders have requested that their traditions not be exploited, sold, or taken out of their proper cultural context. Individuals truly seeking to honor and respect Native traditions, they argue, should thus respect the people from whom such traditions come. To do otherwise is to continue the process of colonization, theft, and disrespect.[3]

The issue of New Age appropriation, felt keenly throughout Native communities across the country, is tied to the notion of intellectual property rights. The application of these rights to Native languages and traditions has become increasingly important in recent years, as Native communities have watched their traditions being appropriated and sold by New Age commercial ventures. Now Native communities are working to protect themselves legally from what they see as cultural theft. This process is complicated by the fact that most Native traditions, until very recently, were maintained through an oral tradition. Elders passed on knowledge to apprenticed young people, who painstakingly learned the narratives, rituals, and prayers appropriate to their spiritual practice. Such knowledge is the property of the community and the culture, not of any single person. Clearly, such a notion of communally held, orally maintained, intellectual property is difficult in the Euroamerican context, where individuals own written, documented information that is copyrighted or patented in their name. This lack of legal protection has, until recently, left Native traditions vulnerable to theft and commodification. The protection of cultural property, from language and oral traditions to ceremonial structures and subsistence activities, will be a centrally important issue for Native peoples in the coming decades. Such protection is not meant to exclude Euroamericans from knowledge about Native cultures and spirituality, but rather to assure that such knowledge is controlled, and properly cared for, by the Native people from whom it comes.[4]

The Hopi Tribe Cultural Preservation Office statement on intellectual property rights helps to illuminate a Native perspective on this issue:

> Through the decades the intellectual property rights of Hopi have been violated for the benefit of many other, non-Hopi

people that has proven to be detrimental ... Although the Hopi believe the ceremonies are intended for the benefit of all people, they also believe benefits only result when ceremonies are properly performed and protected ... through these thefts, sacred rituals have been exposed to others out of context and without Hopi permission. Some of this information has reached individuals for whom it was not intended (e.g., Hopi youth, members of other clans, or non-Hopi).[5]

Many Native leaders share the concerns expressed here: a heartfelt desire to protect their traditions and to see that they are represented faithfully and respectfully.

Related to concerns regarding intellectual property rights is the question of repatriation of human remains and cultural artifacts, and their use as objects of study within a scholarly context. Before 1990, Native dead were not afforded the same legal protections from grave desecration as non-Natives, as federal legislation before that date classified Native American bodies as "archaeological resources" which could be legally collected for study. This approach had a long historical precedent, beginning as early as the Surgeon General's order of 1868, which directed the United States army to collect human remains, particularly crania, for the Army Medical Museum. This led to more than 4,000 heads being taken from burial grounds, hospitals, and battlefields.[6] This interest in collecting human remains stemmed from a belief that Native people were destined to vanish from the earth and that their remains would soon become valuable evidence in the study of the history of the human species. Some nineteenth-century race theories dictated that all races existed on an evolutionary continuum, with Anglo-Saxon Europeans at its peak. Such theories provided justification for the scientific study of human remains without the permission of that individual's family or community, as well as for the forced removal of Native people from their homelands onto reservations. At the same time as they were collecting the dead, collectors began an intensive move to gather cultural materials from Native communities, acquiring ceremonial artifacts for museum collections but also for individual profit. Some materials were acquired through legitimate means, but others were taken through outright theft, were confiscated by missionaries and government agents, or were purchased from individuals who did not have the right, according to indigenous cultural ethics, to sell materials that belonged, in fact, to the wider community.

This historical legacy was not addressed until the 1979 Archaeological Resources Protection Act, which required that archaeologists consult with local Native tribes when undertaking a dig, particularly when human remains were recovered. In 1990, the Native American Graves Protection and Repatriation Act (NAGPRA) was signed into law. The act gave Native communities the legal right to demand the return of human remains and cultural patrimony from public museums and universities. The law, however, did not apply to collections that were privately held.[7]

The continuing implementation of NAGPRA is proving to be one of the most important issues for contemporary Native religious practices in the twenty-first century. The legal process is quite complicated, as is the process of return. Many communities must first build museums to house their repatriated materials, and some must revive indigenous burial traditions that have fallen out of practice. Interpretation of the law is difficult as well, and lawsuits have resulted when conflicts of interest have arisen. One of the most famous of these legal battles centers on Kennewick Man, a 9,600-year-old complete skeleton found on the banks of the Columbia River in Washington State in 1996. The Army Corps of Engineers, who controlled the land on which the skeleton was found, sought to return the remains to Native tribes as soon as its identity was determined. Several physical anthropologists and archaeologists from around the country sued for the remains, however, arguing that their extreme age made them far too valuable to repatriate. The scholars argued that local Native communities (the Confederated Tribes of the Umatilla, the Yakima Indian Nation, the Nez Perce tribe, the Wanapum band, and the Colville Confederated Tribes) had probably not lived in the region 10,000 years earlier, during Kennewick Man's lifetime. These Native nations responded that they had indeed lived in the region for 10,000 years, and that their oral traditions attested to this fact. The tribes fought to have the remains given a proper reburial for, according to their spiritual traditions, it was vitally important that "the Ancient One," as they referred to the remains, be returned to the earth as soon as possible and without further desecration. The lawsuit was further complicated when James Chatters, the archaeologist who first studied the remains, described them to the media as "Caucasoid." The term implies only that the remains had a large nose and oblong face; it does not denote race. But its inclusion in media sources quickly led some to suggest that Caucasian Euroamericans had actually arrived in North America before the ancestors of today's "Native Americans." In February 2004, a federal judge ruled in favor of the anthropologists, and ordered that Kennewick Man be released for study, demonstrating that NAGPRA may be insufficient to protect Native people's religious and cultural concerns.[8]

On the other hand, a growing number of stories describe successful cooperation between anthropologists, archaeologists, and Native communities, in which scholarship and community concerns have been able to work side by side. One of the earliest examples of this was the cooperative effort demonstrated by the trustees of the Denver Art Museum when, in 1977, they agreed to the repatriation of the Zuni War Gods. The icons were gifts to the Zuni people from the Holy People and a source of strength to them as a nation. In their petition, elders pointed to the theft of the sacred War Gods as a cause of current social ills. The Denver Museum agreed to return the sacred objects, along with a donation of $10,000 to aid the Zuni in protecting them.[9] Growing numbers of museums and archaeologists are cultivating new approaches to conducting research, such as including Native consultants on archaeological digs and working to repatriate ceremonial objects and human remains.

Many tribes have also begun their own archaeology programs, working to preserve their past and maintain a role in their own history telling. Archaeologist Larry Zimmerman has long advocated an "indigenous archaeology," which incorporates tribal researchers, oral histories, and partnership between academicians and tribal communities.[10] At the heart of this contemporary approach is a respect for the interests, unique perspectives, and sovereignty of Native nations. As Bruce Stonefish, of the Delaware Nation, recently put it:

> Our oral tradition is our science. When you come to our land, you're going to find our ancestors. That's what you're going to find. When you enter our land, you're entering our relatives. How do you approach the land? Is it a dead thing, so scientific

it's dead? In *Lenapehoking*, our land, we're not going to stand for that. You have to understand, permission has to be asked. We have our research agenda too. We have a way certain things can go. If you don't approach this in a holistic way and understand that, there will be cultural barriers.[11]

Such an approach challenges institutionalized assumptions about history writing and knowledge making, creating a kind of scholarship that gives Native people a role in conceptualizing their own past and mapping their own future. Central to this topic is the notion of semiotic sovereignty, the right and authority of a people to create its own stories, histories, and sense of identity, that is, to craft the semiotics, or symbol systems, of its knowledge.[12]

Legal issues such as intellectual property rights and repatriation are likely to take a prominent role in the expression and continued revival of Native religious practices. At the heart of such legal concerns is the question of sovereignty. Federally recognized Native communities in the United States are sovereign nations with their own

Vi Taqʷšəblu Hilbert, one of the most important contemporary figures within the preservation of Coast Salish culture. She has devoted much of her life to reviving the Coast Salish Lushootseed language and oral traditions.

borders and laws. But this legal relationship is complicated by a history of federal paternalism and control, as well as by what can often be a contentious relationship between tribal and state governments. After more than a century of assimilationist policies (interrupted only by John Collier's brief reforms), government policy made a decisive shift in the late twentieth century, emphasizing the sovereignty of indigenous nations and affirming their rights to self-rule and religious freedom. In the 1974 Indian Self-Determination and Education Assistance Act, Congress gave tribes control over local affairs such as education and health care, a move that Collier had also promoted. The 1978 Indian Child Welfare Act reflected this movement, with the formal end both to mandatory boarding schools and to the federal policy of out-adoption of Native children to non-Native families. In a country founded on principles of religious freedom, it is profoundly ironic that, until the American Indian Religious Freedom Act of 1978, Native people were not ensured the right to practice their indigenous religious traditions. The act guaranteed Native people the "inherent right of freedom to believe, express, and exercise the traditional religions of the American Indian, Eskimo, Aleut, and Native Hawaiians, including but not limited to access to sites, use and possession of sacred objects, and the freedom to worship through ceremonials and traditional rites."[13] Some aspects of religious freedom were still subject to federal control, however, until the 1994 Native American Free Exercise of Religion Act guaranteed indigenous people the right to participate in Native American Church peyote meetings and granted Native American prisoners the right to practice traditional religions within prisons. As Native peoples continue to negotiate their continually changing relationship with the federal government in the decades to come, issues of religious freedom, Native control over religious artifacts, and the repatriation of human remains will continue to be hotly contested issues.

Ecological survival: The Black Hills, Devil's Tower, old growth cedar, and Black Mesa

For Native people working to preserve their cultural and spiritual traditions in the century to come, the protection and restoration of sacred spaces, ecosystems, and habitats present perhaps the most urgent and immediate concerns. As has been emphasized throughout this book, Native American religious traditions emerge from a relationship with an ecological landbase. Subsistence activities, kinship, ritual, ceremony, and storytelling work together to affirm and strengthen a complex system of relationships between individuals, communities, and an animated world filled with sentient spiritual beings. The colonial context has challenged these relationships in profound ways through over-development and environmental destruction, as well as the forcible removal of many Native communities from their traditional homelands. These communities have demonstrated remarkable resilience in adapting and surviving despite this loss. While many Native individuals and communities have been forced to live elsewhere, their original homeland, with its resources and its sacred sites, remains a focal point of spiritual life.

For indigenous spiritual traditions to continue, their sacred sites— be they mountains, rivers, springs, or forests—must survive, and Native people must have access to them. The native food resources that have directly shaped these religious traditions, philosophies, and modes of life must also survive. Without bison, salmon, or corn, Lakota, Salish, and Diné spirituality would be fundamentally transformed. Innumerable sacred spaces are currently at risk from development and resource extraction. Burial locations, areas of subsistence gathering or hunting, and entire sacred mountains are threatened in every region of the country. For brevity's sake, just four specific examples will have to suffice here: the Black Hills, Devil's Tower, old growth stands of cedar, and Black Mesa.[14]

As mentioned in Chapter 2, the Black Hills hold a special place in Lakota oral tradition as the spiritual center for the people, and the place from which the Buffalo Nation emerged. They also contain a number of ceremonial locations that have profound spiritual significance for the Lakota. The First People emerged from the beneath the earth, entering this world through Wind Cave in the southern Black Hills. Referred to as *Paha Sapa*, or "the heart of everything that is," the Black Hills are both a center of ceremonial life and a source of medicine to maintain the physical, mental, and spiritual health of the Lakota people. Ceremonies are conducted throughout the Black Hills from early spring to the end of summer. Although the area was set aside for the Lakota in the 1868 Fort Laramie Treaty, which established the borders of the Great Sioux Reservation, these borders were violated once gold was discovered there. The United States government sought to convince the Lakota to sell the Black Hills, but the U.S. was able to acquire a treaty signed by only 10% of the adult male population, not even close to the number required for legal ratification. Nonetheless, the government seized the land. A century later, in 1975, the U.S. Court of Claims ruled on the theft of the Black Hills, stating that "a more ripe and rank case of dishonourable dealings will never, in all probability, be found in our history."[15] In 1980, the Indian Claims Commission and the Supreme Court both ruled that the taking of the Black Hills from the Lakota people was indeed a theft. Rather than require the return of the land to the people, however, the court offered the Lakota financial compensation for their loss. The Lakota people refused to take money for lands they deemed sacred, and in refusing the money sought to retain their right of ownership. Today, over $570 million dollars sits in an account set up by the United States government, but the Lakota people continue to refuse to accept it.

Since the late nineteenth century, despite protests by the Lakota people, the Black Hills have been subject to mining, logging, and extensive recreational development. Mining has polluted water and devastated the landscape, and many mining companies have been permitted to avoid any environmental clean-up. East of the Black Hills, Bear Butte is a particularly important location for Lakota ceremonies, vision quests, and gatherings, but today it has become a popular tourist destination, despite requests by the Lakota and Cheyenne that tourist access be restricted during times of ceremonial activities. Forest Service officials have requested that hikers avoid the area, but these restrictions are not enforced.

While the American Indian Religious Freedom Act (1978) ensured access to sacred sites, the act had no teeth with which to protect these sites or Native access to them. Mining companies are still allowed to extract resources from the Black Hills without any obligation to clean up pollution or restore the land, and today less than 1% of the Black Hills is protected from logging and resource extraction.

Devil's Tower in Wyoming is another location sacred to the Lakota and other Northern Plains people. For centuries it has been the location of vision quests, Sun Dances, and prayer. In the contemporary era, Devil's Tower has also become a favorite spot for rock climbing. After climbers disturbed sacred ceremonies, Native communities protested and petitioned the National Park Service for protection of this sacred area. Park Service officials sought to find a compromise, and requested the climbers not to venture onto the natural monument during the month of June, when ceremonies are under way. Most climbers (about 85%) gracefully agreed, seeking other locations for their sport during this month. Some, however, acting under the auspices of the Mountain States Legal Foundation, challenged the request, seeing it as an unconstitutional establishment of religion by a federal governing body. The group argues that climbing is, for them, a religious activity, and that they have as much right to climb the monument as Native people do to conduct ceremonies near it. The dilemma at Devil's Tower and the attempts to find a compromise may well establish a precedent, for such conflicts between recreational users and indigenous ceremonials are likely to increase in the coming decades, as more and more people compete for less and less undeveloped space, and as secular and religious ideologies continue to come into conflict.

Such conflicts can be seen in the Pacific Northwest as well, where demands on old growth cedar forests, both for recreation and for timber harvesting, have threatened the spiritual traditions of Coast Salish people. As Gerald B. Miller, traditional spiritual leader of the Skokomish tribe, has explained:

> Our concern is that the destruction of these precious resources will jeopardize the instructional process we use to pass on traditional knowledge to younger generations and to help maintain the order of existence. For example, traditional elders educate younger tribal members about their culture by seeking a guardian spirit in the vast expanse of old-growth forest, gathering plants and preparing medicine, and explaining the role of such entities as water and animals in our life. These practices are threatened because the forest is dwindling, the plants are dying, and few people respect our beliefs about such entities as water and animals.[16]

Cedar in particular plays an important role in the spiritual life of the Skokomish tribe, because of the careful ecological balance necessary for cedar forests to thrive, and because cedar had been chosen by the Great Spirit to guide, instruct, and counsel human beings, offering them wisdom and insight into the proper way to live in balance with other living beings in the world. Cedar gives the Skokomish people all the fundamental tools of survival: her bark provides material for clothing and basketry, her wood provides material for housing, tools, and canoes. Cedar is credited with having given the people some of their most important ceremonies: those to honor first berries and first roots, and the First Salmon ceremony as well. Skokomish oral traditions tell of a time when a young girl was transformed into a salmon, traveling to the home of the Chum Salmon people, where she married the son of the chief of the Chum Salmon. When she and her children returned to her village, it was Cedar that transformed them back into the people, the ancestors of the Skokomish. As Pavel, Miller, and Pavel have argued: "Protecting the environment is essential, because the Skokomish spiritual philosophy focuses not on events but on relationships with entities like earth, water, air, animals, and plant people. Maintaining this symbolic connection is important to the survival of our traditional culture, because a spiritual relationship with other life forms pervades all aspects of our life."[17]

In the American Southwest, resource extraction has also challenged the sustainability of Diné and Hopi spirituality. According to environmental groups and Native American observers, a coalmine has devastated Black Mesa, a region estimated to hold over 2,000 archaeological sites and currently home to 16,000 Diné and 8,000 Hopi people. Ground water and desert springs are threatened by the mining, which pumps 3 million gallons of water a day for use in the slurry line. Black Mesa has the only coal slurry line operating in the United States, because of the method's destructive impact on the environment and threat to water supplies. According to the social justice group Black Mesa Indigenous Support, thousands of Diné have been forcibly removed from their homes to make way for the mine, but many still cling to their land, even after their homes have been bulldozed. Judith Nies reported that in the 1980s, when Diné leaders traveled to Washington D.C. to protest the removal, they went unheard. According to Nies, the president of Peabody Coal

Mining Company, which had owned the mine, served on President Reagan's energy advisory board, and Peabody's new parent company, Bechtel, was a part of Washington's political elite: George Schultz, Bechtel's former president, was Secretary of State; Secretary of Defence Caspar Weinberger was Bechtel's former legal counsel; and Ken Davis, Assistant Secretary of Energy, had previously been director of Bechtel Nuclear.[18]

The cultural survival of the Hopi and Diné is directly challenged by the desecration of Black Mesa. Their spiritual traditions are built on a contractual agreement between the people and the Creator. The Creator gave the people life and an abundant landscape; in return, the people must maintain and protect that landscape. In 1966 the Hopi and Diné tribal councils, acting without any tribal referendum, signed leases opening Black Mesa to Peabody Coal. Since then, more than 12,000 Diné people have been removed from their homes, the largest Indian removal since the 1880s. Today, in what is misleadingly referred to as the "Navajo–Hopi land dispute," the people are fighting the lease, seeking both an end to the mining before ground water resources and the ecosystem itself are irreparably damaged and an end to the forced relocation of Hopi and Diné people from land on which they have lived cooperatively and sustainably for countless generations.[19]

Success stories in the effort to protect sacred land can be pointed to as well: agreements have been made to share recreational locations such as the nearly successful example at Devil's Tower. One can also point to the example of Mount Shasta in northern California. When developers proposed to build a ski run on the mountain, Native communities and environmental groups protested, arguing that the summit was a location of sacred activities for northern California Indians. Forest Service officials responded to the Native community's concerns by rejecting the developers' proposal. Additional successes have come in the realm of species restoration, such as efforts to restore salmon and salmon habitat in the Pacific Northwest. There is also the example of Zuni Salt Lake in west central New Mexico. The inland salt lake had been a sacred site for the Zuni Pueblo since time immemorial, holding spiritual and subsistence significance for many Native communities in the Southwest. For over twenty years, the Arizona electric power company Salt River Project (SRP), which provides power to most of Phoenix and its surrounding environment, had planned to develop a coal strip mine near the lake. Strip mining, since it destroys underground aquifers, would have directly threatened the lake. Years of political activism by the Zuni Salt Lake Coalition was eventually successful, and the SRP dropped its plans for a mine in August 2003.

Other success stories take the form of protecting animal species. After the U.S. cavalry's nearly successful effort to exterminate them in the nineteenth century, bison have now returned to the Plains. Much of this success has to do with the efforts of Native nations and organizations such as the InterTribal Bison Cooperative (ITBC), formed in 1992. This effort differed from similar non-Native efforts in that it emphasized the reintroduction of bison into the spiritual, economic, and cultural lives of Native communities. Fifty Plains tribes currently belong to the organization, which promotes a notion of a "spiritual economy." Here traditional religious practices are incorporated alongside contemporary wildlife management. The ITBC promotes the notion of bison as a sustainable resource, and one that promotes the physical and spiritual well-being of Plains people. The ITBC believes that, if treated with reverence and respect, bison herds can again come to play a central role in the spiritual economy of the region. The traditional spiritual approach to the bison, which is being put into practice, is being carried out with a remarkably contemporary look. The Lakota tribe at Cheyenne River in northern South Dakota, for instance, is a member of the ITBC, and holds the largest tribal bison herd in the United States. A tribally owned non-profit corporation manages the bison herd, which exceeds 2,500 head. The tribe has acquired 42,000 acres of grassland on which to raise the growing herds. Guiding the tribe's work is a sense that the renewal of native bison herds is essential to any community efforts toward ecological, economic, and cultural restoration. Even the slaughtering of the animals has taken a distinctly traditional–contemporary expression. Before being killed, animals must be thanked and honored for their gift of life. Slaughterhouses, it was argued, distress the animals and are not conducive to ceremonial activities. In response, the ITBC created a portable slaughterhouse, which adheres to federal regulations for meatpacking but also allows the bison to be killed on the open Plains and with proper ritual acknowledgement.[20]

During the 1960s Pacific Northwest tribal nations and communities staged "fish-ins," intended to protest fishing regulations that they argued violated their treaty rights. In this photo, taken on March 2, 1964, actor Marlon Brando stands alongside Puyallup tribal leader Bob Satiacum, just before Brando's arrest during a fish-in.

Efforts to restore bison populations are being matched by efforts to restore salmon populations in the Northwest, where the fish are central to Native economies, diet, and spirituality. The fish-ins of the 1960s helped to establish Native groups' right to fish, and since that time Native communities have also taken responsibility for safeguarding fish populations and their habitat. One example of this is the Northwest Indian Fisheries Commission (NWIFC), an organization established in 1974 by the twenty treaty tribes of western Washington, which works to manage fisheries and salmon conservation in the region. Another example is the Columbia River Inter-Tribal Fish Commission (CRITFC), a coalition of the Yakima, Warm Springs, Umatilla, and Nez Perce nations that works to ensure that salmon are respected and treated in accordance with their sacred status. The CRITFC manages a number of fisheries and advocates for habitat restoration and protection of Native treaty rights over nearly 150 miles of the Columbia River, as well as assisting in watershed restoration and policy development. The commission also helped to start Salmon Corps, an Americorps project for Native young people. Salmon Corps focuses on renewing habitat and healthy salmon runs; it and similar tribal efforts have shown great success in restoring runs of salmon to rivers and watersheds where salmon species have not been seen in decades. As Executive Director Donald Sampson explained: "In return for the salmon sacrificing their body for us to live, we were obligated to take care of them. That is our obligation as Indian people: to be their caretakers. ... [The CRITFC has] seen rivers where there were no fish where fish have been restored. ... They've seen treaty rights protected. They've seen people start to respect salmon."[21]

And, as was described in Chapter 1, as salmon populations fight for their survival, tribes throughout the Northwest have revived First Salmon ceremonies, celebrating the return of salmon each spring. In doing so, the community is reminded of the important role that the surrounding ecosystem plays in their cultural and spiritual inheritance. Such ceremonials are a way of educating Native young people and Euroamerican visitors of the intricate balance that ties creation together, and of the importance of maintaining a sense of respect for and reciprocity with the natural world.

Members of groups such as the ITBC, NWIFC, and CRITFC point to health and dietary concerns as one of the reasons why Native people need salmon and bison restored. With the imposition of the reservation system, Native people were given a diet of commodity foods and rations, foods that were high in starch, simple sugars, and fat. The result has been an epidemic of obesity and diabetes throughout Indian Country. The sedentary lifestyle of many reservations has added to this risk, increasing rates of cancer and heart disease. Traditional Native cultures were marked by active lifestyles of hunting and gathering, and traditional food resources were healthy and varied. Bison, for instance, is high in protein and iron, and very low in fat and cholesterol, in contrast to grain-fed livestock such as beef and pork, which are high in fat. Many tribal communities throughout the country are now promoting a return to traditional foods and the healthy lifestyles that accompanied them. As has been emphasized in this book, traditional food resources play a central role in indigenous religious life. To restore bison or salmon to a tribal community is most often also to restore important elements of traditional spirituality. As one woman on the Pine Ridge Reservation observed: "This approach to diabetes isn't just about food. When you bring back the knowledge and skills about preparing food, you bring back the ceremonies that go with them. Maybe this is a message from the Creator that we have to hang on to those traditions to survive in the next century."[22]

Conclusion: Toward a global indigeneity

This book offers a glimpse into Native American religious and cultural life, its diversity, its challenges, and its successes. The twenty-first century presents profound challenges to Native people, especially to their cultural and ecological survival. Challenges to Native intellectual property rights come from New Age authors and merchandisers who take Native traditions out of their context, distort their message, and at times make public elements of Native ceremonies or rituals that are meant to be private. Native communities also face legal battles related to repatriation of artifacts and human remains and to the protection of tribal sovereignty. Resource extraction, land development, and inappropriate recreational use also pose great threats to the survival of archaeological sites and ceremonial locations; court battles continue today to protect such locations or to set aside times of year for the private ceremonial use of Native people. Unlike most contemporary religious practices, the majority of traditional Native religious practices are not portable; they are place-bound and dependent on access to specific locations. Many Native nations, particularly those forcibly removed from their homeland (such as the Cherokee), have adapted to the loss of landscape, transforming their cultures in ways that maintained core traditional values, reshaped to fit a new context. Such examples testify to the strength of Native cultural systems while demonstrating the devastating effect loss of land can have in a tradition built on a relationship with that landscape. The loss of sacred sites directly threatens the continuity of indigenous spiritual practices. Native religious life hinges on a relationship with the landscape, in particular with the food resources that have defined indigenous economies and spiritualities for millennia. It is vital that these ecosystems and endangered species survive, if Native religious traditions are to survive as well.

Native religious traditions outlasted the threats of the nineteenth century: reservations, missionary zeal, and the outright banning of indigenous ceremonies. These same communities are responding to contemporary challenges. Nations are petitioning for the repatriation of cultural patrimony under NAGPRA and are fighting for the protection of sacred sites. Tribal coalitions are working together to protect forests, restore salmon habitat, and return native bison herds to the Great Plains.

Such efforts are not merely local, however, but are also taking place on a global scale. Native communities are discovering that their concerns are mirrored in the experiences of indigenous people around the world. Guarding indigenous sovereignty and intellectual property rights, protecting and restoring ecosystems and traditional subsistence activities, and cultivating a restoration of traditional cultures and languages are goals shared by Native people throughout the world. The approximately 370 million indigenous people worldwide share in common issues as well as common histories of colonialism and human rights abuses.

The increasing presence of indigenous peoples within the United Nations is a clear indicator of the growing trend toward global cooperation and involvement. In 1982, the United Nations Economic and Social Council established the Working Group on Indigenous Populations. The group drafted a declaration of the rights of indigenous peoples, a document currently under discussion in the United Nations, with the goal of protecting their individual and collective rights. In 1993, the second World Conference on Human Rights in Vienna emphasized the responsibility of U.N. member states to honor the human rights of indigenous peoples. The following year marked the beginning of the International Decade of the World's Indigenous Peoples, a decade that concludes as this book is being written. Throughout the past ten years, U.N. agencies have worked with indigenous groups to create and put into practice projects focused on the protection of indigenous communities and their health, education, housing, and employment, placing particular emphasis on the integration of religious traditions and cultural values within these projects. Indigenous rights groups maintained a strong presence and participation in other international gatherings as well, including the Earth Summit in Rio de Janeiro in 1992, the World Conference on Women in Beijing in 1995, the Social Summit in 1996, and the World Conference against Racism in Durban, South Africa, in 2001.

One primary goal of the United Nations' Decade was the creation of the Permanent Forum on Indigenous Issues, which officially began in April 2000. The forum is charged to provide advice and recommendations to the United Nations Economic and Social Council, to promote awareness and coordination of activities that relate to indigenous concerns as they take place in the United Nations, and to collect and disseminate information on indigenous issues. Its first meeting was held in May 2002.

The U.N. Forum on Indigenous Issues is perhaps the most visible of a growing number of international alliances among indigenous people as they work to meet the growing challenges of the coming millennium. The history of colonialism that indigenous people have experienced is one marked by brutality, tragedy, and conflict. But it is also one of remarkable resilience, in which Native communities have worked with each other, and with non-Natives, to preserve indigenous human rights and economic and political sovereignty, and to maintain their cultural and spiritual lives. Native people in North America have overcome enormous obstacles to find themselves today in what many see as an era of cultural and political renaissance. Native communities are growing in strength, reviving classical religious practices, and exerting a growing political strength in the protection of natural resources.

Notes

Chapter 1

1   An excellent listing can be found at:
    http://www.kstrom.net/isk/maps/tribesnonrec.html.

2   It should be noted that Coast Salish refers to a cultural and linguistic group that
    includes a wide range of Native nations extending from British Columbia to the
    Oregon coast, communities that share a common language, landscape, and spiritual
    traditions, but that differ in terms of some specific ceremonial practices, linguistic
    dialects, and oral traditions. Coast Salish nations include: the Nuxalk, Homalco,
    Klahoose, Sliammon, Sechelth, Squamish, Halq'emeylem, Ostlq'emeylem,
    Hul'qumi'num, Pentlatch, Straits, Klallum, Quileute, Puyallup, Nisqually, Chehalis,
    Squaxin Island, Skokomish, and Tillamook.

3   Both the terms "American Indian" and "Native American" are problematic in nature
    and origin. Seeing "Indian" as a clear misnomer, evocative of a colonial history, many
    scholars and activists have chosen to use "Native American" as a more sensitive term.
    However, this makes use of another Euroamerican moniker, "American," to describe
    a people and homeland that had existed long before it was mapped out as "America."
    And indeed, the situation is complicated all the more when it is considered that most
    contemporary indigenous people of the United States refer to themselves as "Indian,"
    reappropriating a term that mislabeled them for centuries. Indigenous peoples of
    Canada, on the other hand, have taken up the term "First Peoples" or "First Nations"
    to describe themselves. In this book, I will use the terms American Indian, Native
    American, and Native interchangeably to refer to the indigenous people of what is
    now known as North America. However, whenever possible, I will refer to the nations
    in question by their own names for themselves, preferring to emphasize the distinct
    and individual traditions, rather than attempting to describe a mythical and
    monolithically "Indian religion."

4   Information for this description was gathered from the following sources: Leonard
    Crow Dog, *Crow Dog: Four Generations of Sioux Medicine Men* (New York:
    HarperCollins, 1996); Diane Glancy, "Sun Dance," in *Native American Religious
    Identity,* Jace Weaver, ed. (Maryknoll: Orbis, 1998); John Grim, "Sun Dance," in
    American Indian Religious Traditions: An Encyclopedia, Suzanne Crawford and
    Dennis Kelley, eds. (Oxford: ABC–Clio, 2005); Howard L. Harrod, *Renewing the
    World: Plains Indian Religion and Morality* (Tucson: University of Arizona Press,
    1987); Thomas E. Mails, *Sundancing at Rosebud and Pine Ridge* (Sioux Falls: Center
    for Western Studies, Augustana College, 1978); Leslie Spier, "The Sun Dance of the
    Plains Indians: Its Development and Diffusion," *Anthropological Papers of the
    American Museum of Natural History,* Vol. 16, Pt. 7, pp. 449–527; New York: The
    Trustees of the American Museum of Natural History, 1921; James Walker, Raymond
    J. DeMallie, and Elaine A. Jahner, eds., *Lakota Belief and Ritual* (Lincoln: University
    of Nebraska Press, 1980); Thomas Yellowtail, *Yellowtail: Crow Medicine Man and
    Sun Dance Chief,* as told to Michael O. Fitzgerald (Norman: University of Oklahoma
    Press, 1991). For an excellent online bibliography, see
    http://puffin.creighton.edu/lakota/biblio.htm.

5   Marla N. Powers, *Oglala Women* (Chicago: University of Chicago Press, 1983), pp. 72–3.

6   Mary Crow Dog, *Lakota Woman* (New York: HarperCollins, 1990), p. 260.

7   This description is an amalgam of Coast Salish First Salmon ceremonies as they occur
    throughout the Puget Sound region. Slight details vary from community to

community, but the overall structure and intent remain the same. Information for this section was drawn from personal observations, personal communications, and the following publications: Erna Gunther, *An Analysis of the First Salmon Ceremony* (Seattle: University of Washington Publications in Anthropology, 1926); Erna Gunther, *A Further Analysis of the First Salmon Ceremony* (Seattle: University of Washington Publications in Anthropology, 1928); Christian Hill, "Squaxin Welcome Salmon Season with Ritual Return," *The Olympian* (June, 2003); Karen McCowan, "Tribal Elder Keeps Salmon Ceremony Going Strong," *Eugene, Oregon Register Guard* (June 20, 2004); Cathy McDonald, "Tulalip Tribal Members Show their Respect for Salmon," *The Seattle Times* (June 24, 2004); and Kari Thorene Shaw, "Salmon Ceremony Reflects Culture, Struggle," *The Bellingham Herald* (June 1, 2001).

8   For further reading on the *Kinààldá*, see: Shirley Begay et al., *Kinààldá: A Navajo Puberty Ceremony* (Phoenix, AZ: Navajo Curriculum Center, 1983); Charlotte Johnson Frisbie, *Kinààldá: A Study of the Navajo Girls' Puberty Ceremony* (Salt Lake City: University of Utah Press, 1993); and Maureen Trudelle Schwarz, *Molded in the Image of Changing Woman: Navajo Views on the Human Body and Personhood* (Tucson: University of Arizona Press, 1997).

Chapter 2

1   Other books in this Religions of the World series are organized on a linear–historical model. Following such a model, this chapter would address ancient or prehistoric origins of these traditions. I prefer to avoid this Euroamerican approach to Native traditions, because it does not reflect the ways in which traditional Native cultures describe and perceive their history. As many scholars have already pointed out (see Keith Basso, *Wisdom Sits in Places: Landscape and Language among the Weston Apache* [Albuquerque: University of New Mexico Press, 1996]), indigenous notions of history are not linear but place-based, circular, and intrinsically present-centered. History is contemporary, and a living part of contemporary life. To that end, rather than discussing the origins of these traditions as if they were long ago and not a part of contemporary practice, I instead describe the philosophical foundations of these religious practices and beliefs, as they are found within Native oral traditions.

2   For further reading on Lakota oral traditions, see Mark St. Pierre and Tilda Long Soldier, *Walking in the Sacred Manner* (New York: Simon and Schuster, 1995); James R. Walker, *Lakota Myth* (Lincoln: University of Nebraska Press, 1983); and Severt Young Bear, *Standing in the Light: A Lakota Way of Seeing* (Lincoln: University of Nebraska Press, 1994).

3   James R. Walker, Raymond J. De Maille, and Elaine A. Jahner (eds.), *Lakota Belief and Ritual* (Lincoln: University of Nebraska Press, 1980), p. 50.

4   See Walker 1991.

5   See Martin Brokenleg, "Ceremony and Ritual, Lakota," in *American Indian Religious Traditions: An Encyclopedia*, ed. Suzanne Crawford and Dennis Kelley (Denver, Oxford: ABC–Clio, 2005); Marla N. Powers, *Oglala Women: Myth, Ritual, and Reality* (Chicago: University of Chicago Press, 1983); William K. Powers, *Oglala Religion* (Lincoln: University of Nebraska Press, 1977); Walker 1991.

6   Ella Cara Deloria, *Speaking of Indians* (Vermillion: Dakota Press, 1979).

7   For further reading on Coast Salish pre-colonial traditions, see Thelma Adamson, *Folk-Tales of the Coast Salish* (New York: G.E. Techert and Co., 1934); Pamela Amoss and William Seaburg, eds., *Badger and Coyote Were Neighbors: Melville Jacobs on Northwest Coast Myths and Tales* (Eugene: University of Oregon Press, 2000); Wayne Suttles, *Coast Salish Essays* (Seattle: University of Washington Press, 1987); and Wayne Suttles, ed., *Handbook of North American Indians: Northwest Coast* (Washington D.C.: Smithsonian Press, 1990).

8   D. Michael Pavel, Gerald B. Miller, and Mary J. Pavel, "Too Long Too Silent: The Threat to Cedar and the Sacred Ways of the Skokomish," *American Indian Culture and Research Journal*, 17/3 (1993), p. 56. See also, "Mink and the Changer," in Vi Hilbert, *Haboo: Native American Stories from Puget Sound* (Seattle: University of Washington Press, 1985), pp. 57–69.

9   See Pamela Amoss, *Coast Salish Spirit Dancing: The Survival of an Ancestral Religion* (Seattle: University of Washington Press, 1978) and Suttles 1987.

10   See Amoss 1978, p. 42.

11   While rarely practiced today, spirit quests have survived in various forms among some Coast Salish communities (Amoss 1978).

12   See Pavel, Miller, and Pavel 1993, p. 54.

13   See Suttles 1987.

14   For resources on the potlatch traditions, see Sergei Kan, *Symbolic Immortality: The Tlingit Potlatch of the Nineteenth Century* (Washington D.C.: Smithsonian Press, 1989); Amoss 1978; and Suttles 1987.

15   Amoss 1978, pp. 46–56, 60–63.

16   See, for example, Franz Boas, *Kwakiutl Religion* (New York: Columbia University Press, 1930); Philip Drucker, *Cultures of the North Pacific Coast* (San Francisco: Chandler, 1965); and Stanley Walens, *Feasting with Cannibals: An Essay on Kwakiutl Cosmology* (Princeton: Princeton University Press, 1981).

17   For further examples see Boas 1930; Franz Boas, *Kwakiutl Tales* (New York: Columbia University Press, 1910); Drucker 1965; Erna Gunther, "Analysis of the First Salmon Ceremony," *American Anthropologist*, 28 (1926), pp. 605–17; Erna Gunther, *A Further Analysis of the First Salmon Ceremony* (Seattle: University of Washington Publications in Anthropology 2, no. 5, 1928), pp. 129–73.

18   For further reading on the Spirit Canoe ceremony, see Jay Miller, *Shamanic Odyssey: The Lushootseed Salish Journey to the Land of the Dead* (Menlo Park: Ballena Press, 1989); and Jay Miller, *Lushootseed Culture and Shamanic Odyssey: An Anchored Radiance* (Lincoln: University of Nebraska Press, 1999).

19   Miller 1989, and 1999.

20   Information in this section has been adapted from Gladys Reichard, *Navajo Religion* (Princeton: Princeton University Press, 1990).

21   James K. McNeley, *Holy Wind in Navajo Philosophy* (Tucson: University of Arizona Press, 1981). For other creation accounts see Jerrold Levy, *In the Beginning: The Navajo Genesis* (Berkeley: University of California Press, 1998); Reichard 1990; Paul Zobrod, *Dine Bahane: The Navajo Creation Story* (Albuquerque: University of New Mexico, 1988).

22   Father Berard Haile, *Women Versus Men: A Conflict of Navajo Emergence* (Lincoln: University of Nebraska Press, 1981).

23   Reichard 1990, p. 20, chart 1.

24   The account that follows is adapted from McNeley 1981.

25   See John R. Farella, *The Main Stalk: A Synthesis of Navajo Religion* (Tucson: University of Arizona Press, 1984).

26   See Farella 1984.

27   McNeley 1981, p. 35.

28   McNeley 1981, p. 36.

29   See Charlotte Frisbie, ed., *Southwestern Indian Ritual Drama* (Long Grove, IL: Waveland Press, 1989).

Chapter 3

1   For further background on early missionary movements in North America, see James Axtell, *The Invasion Within: The Conquest of Cultures in Colonial North America* (Oxford: Oxford University Press, 1986).

2   For further reading on the emergence of federal assimilation programs, see Frederick
    Hoxie, *A Final Promise: The Campaign to Assimilate the Indians, 1880–1920*
    (Lincoln: University of Nebraska Press, 2001).
3   See John Ehle, *Trail of Tears: The Rise and Fall of the Cherokee Nation* (New York:
    Anchor, 1997); Anthony F. C. Wallace, *The Long, Bitter Trail: Andrew Jackson and
    the Indians* (New York: Hill and Wang, 1993); Theda Perdue and Michael D. Green,
    eds., *The Cherokee Removal: A Brief History with Documents* (New York: Bedford
    Books of St. Martin's Press, 1995); and Pamela Jean Owens, "The Trail of Tears,"
    in *American Indian Religious Traditions: An Encyclopedia* (Denver, Oxford:
    ABC–Clio, 2005).
4   The Bureau of Indian Affairs was established by Congress on March 11, 1824. It was
    originally located in the War Department, but was moved to the Department of the
    Interior in 1949. The bureau's responsibility is the administration and managing of
    lands held by the U.S. government in trust for Native Americans and Alaska Natives
    and the administration of health and human services and economic development.
5   See Hoxie 2002.
6   It may be worth noting that such reformers were largely upper middle-class
    Protestants from New England, many of whom had been ante-bellum abolitionists.
7   See Hoxie 2002.
8   Lee Irwin, "Freedom, Law, and Prophecy: A Brief History of Native American
    Religious Resistance," in *Native American Spirituality* (Lincoln: Bison Books, 2000),
    p. 296.
9   Allotment policies were implemented gradually and, in some areas such as the desert
    southwest, not at all. Hence, some regions today have larger and more viable
    reservation communities than others. For further information on allotment policies,
    see Hoxie 2002.
10 See Kenneth R. Philip, *John Collier's Crusade for Indian Reform, 1920–1954*
    (Tucson: University of Arizona Press, 1977).
11 For further discussion on the influence of missions, see Henry Warner Bowden,
    American Indians and Christian Missions: Studies in Cultural Conflict (Chicago:
    University of Chicago, 1985).
12 See Anthony Wallace, *Death and Rebirth of the Seneca* (New York: Vintage Books,
    1972).
13 See Richard White, *The Middle Ground: Indians, Empires and Republics in the
    Great Lakes Region, 1650–1815* (Cambridge: Cambridge University Press, 1991),
    pp. 502–22.
14 The Lakota had already signed other treaties with the United States government,
    including the treaties of 1825 and 1851.
15 For further reading on the Ghost Dance, see Alice Kehoe Beck, *The Ghost Dance:
    Ethnohistory and Revitalization* (Washington, D.C.: International Thompson
    Publishing, 1997); Michael Hittman, *Wovoka and the Ghost Dance* (Lincoln:
    University of Nebraska Press, 1998); and James Mooney, *The Ghost Dance Religion
    and the Sioux Outbreak of 1890* (Lincoln: University of Nebraska Press, 1991).
16 See Stanley Vestal, *New Sources of Indian History, 1850–1891: The Ghost Dance:
    The Prairie Sioux, A Miscellany* (Norman: University of Oklahoma Press, 1934), p. 9.
17 Dee Brown, *Bury My Heart at Wounded Knee: An Indian History of the American
    West* (New York: Henry Hold and Co., 2001); James Mooney, *The Ghost Dance
    Religion and Wounded Knee* (Mineola, NY: Dover, 1991).
18 See Raymond DeMallie, *The Sixth Grandfather: Black Elk's Teachings to John G.
    Neihardt* (Lincoln: University of Nebraska Press, 1985), p. 294. This quotation comes
    from the direct transcript of Black Elk's words, in Raymond DeMallie's *The Sixth
    Grandfather*. Neihardt reinterpreted Black Elk's story, telling it as a tragic epic,
    culminating in tragic defeat and the destruction of Native culture. His inclination to

view the scene tragically made him rephrase Black Elk's words considerably. Where Black Elk said the words quoted above, Neihardt, in *Black Elk Speaks*, rewrote it thus: "And I, to whom so great a vision was given in my youth—you see me now a pitiful old man who has done nothing, for the nation's hoop is broken and scattered. There is no center any longer, the sacred tree is dead." John G. Neihardt, *Black Elk Speaks* (Lincoln: Bison Books, 2003), p. 207.

19 See Robert Boyd, *The Coming of the Spirit of Pestilence: Introduced Infectious Diseases and Population Decline among Northwest Coast Indians, 1774–1874* (Vancouver: University of British Columbia, 1999).

20 See Sergei Kan, *Symbolic Immortality: The Tlingit Potlatch of the 19th Century* (Washington D.C.: Smithsonian Press, 1989); and Douglas Cole and Ira Chaikin, *An Iron Hand Upon the People: The Law Against the Potlatch on the Northwest Coast* (Seattle: University of Washington Press, 1990).

21 The Indian Shaker Church has no connection with the New England sect founded by Mother Ann Lee, and referred to as the Shakers (but more properly known as United Society of Believers).

22 H.G. Barnett, *Indian Shakers: A Messianic Cult of the Pacific Northwest* (Carbondale, IL: Southern Illinois University Press, 1972); Robert H. Ruby and John Brown, *John Slocum and the Indian Shaker Church* (Norman: University of Oklahoma Press, 1996).

23 See Barnett 1972.

24 Barnett 1972.

25 George Pierre Castille, ed., *The Indians of Puget Sound: The Notebooks of Myron Eells.* (Seattle: University of Washington Press, 1985).

26 See Andrew Knaut, *The Pueblo Revolt of 1680: Conquest and Resistance in Seventeenth Century New Mexico* (Norman: University of Oklahoma Press, 1997).

27 Clyde Kluckhohn and Dorothea Leighton, *The Navajo* (Cambridge, MA: Harvard University Press, 1992).

28 See John Adair and Kurt Deuschle, *The People's Health: Anthropology and Medicine in a Navajo Community* (New York: Meredith Corp., 1970); Robert A. Trennert, *White Man's Medicine: Government Doctors and the Navajo, 1863–1955* (Albuquerque: University of New Mexico, 1998).

29 See also Lori Alvord, *The Scalpel and the Silver Bear: The First Navajo Woman Surgeon Combines Western Medicine and Traditional Healing* (New York: Bantam, 2000).

Chapter 4

1 See Troy Johnson, *The Occupation of Alcatraz Island: Indian Self Determination and the Rise of Indian Activism* (Champaign: University of Illinois Press, 1996).

2 For a firsthand account of the siege, and of the events that preceded and followed it, read Mary Crow Dog's *Lakota Woman* (New York: HarperCollins, 1990). Mary, who later became the wife of Leonard Crow Dog, gave birth to a son during the occupation of Wounded Knee.

3 For information on the legal basis for Native fishing rights, see Fay Cohen, *Treaties on Trial: The Continuing Controversy over Northwest Indian Fishing Rights* (Seattle: University of Washington Press, 1986).

4 See Cohen 1986.

5 See Huston Smith, ed., *One Nation under God: The Triumph of the Native American Church* (Santa Fe: Clear Light Publishing, 1996).

6 See Jennifer Denetdale, "Native American Church, Diné," in *American Indian Religious Traditions: An Encyclopedia* (Denver, Oxford: ABC–Clio, 2005).

7 See Elizabeth L. Lewton and Victoria Bydone, "Identity Healing in Three Navajo

Religious Traditions: Sa'ah Naaghai Bik'eh Hozho," *Medical Anthropology Quarterly*, 14/4 (2000), pp. 476–97.

8   For further reading on Lakota ceremonialism, see Martin Brokenleg, "Ceremony and Ritual, Lakota," in *American Indian Religious Traditions: An Encyclopedia*, ed. Suzanne Crawford and Dennis Kelley (Denver, Oxford: ABC–Clio, 2005).

9   Brokenleg 2005.

10 See also Raymond Bucko, *The Lakota Ritual of the Sweat Lodge: History and Contemporary Practice* (Lincoln: University of Nebraska Press, 1998).

11 For a description, see Mark St. Pierre, *Madonna Swan: A Lakota Woman's Story* (Norman: University of Oklahoma Press, 1994).

12 See also Paul Steinmetz, *Pipe, Bible, and Peyote among the Oglala Lakota: A Study in Religious Identity* (Syracuse: Syracuse University Press, 1998).

13 See, for example, Pamela Amoss, *Coast Salish Spirit Dancing: The Survival of an Ancestral Religion* (Seattle: University of Washington Press, 1978) and Crisca Bierwert, *Brushed by Cedar, Living by the River: Coast Salish Figures of Power* (Tucson: University of Arizona Press, 1999).

14 See Amoss 1978.

15 See Bierwert 1999.

16 See also Wayne Suttles, *Coast Salish Essays* (Seattle: University of Washington Press, 1987).

17 See Amoss 1978.

18 See Maureen Trudelle Schwarz, *Molded in the Image of Changing Woman: Navajo Views on the Human Body and Personhood* (Tucson: University of Arizona Press, 1997).

19 For discussions of Navajo/Diné Chantways, see Charlotte Frisbie, ed., *Southwestern Indian Ritual Drama* (Long Grove, IL: Waveland Press, 1989); and Trudy Griffin-Pierce, "The Continuous Renewal of Sacred Relations: Navajo Religion," in *Native Religions and Cultures of North America: Anthropology of the Sacred* (New York: Continuum Press, 2000).

20 See Nancy Parezo, *Navajo Sandpainting: From Ceremonial Act to Commercial Art* (Albuquerque: University of New Mexico Press, reprint edition, 1991); and Leland Wyman, *Southwest Indian Drypainting* (Albuquerque: University of New Mexico Press, 1983).

21 See Trudy Griffin-Pierce, *Earth is My Mother, Sky is My Father: Space, Time, and Astronomy in Navajo Sandpainting* (Albuquerque: University of New Mexico Press, 1995); and Nancy Parezo, "Sandpaintings," and "Ceremony and Ritual, Navajo (Diné)," in *American Indian Religious Traditions: An Encyclopedia*, ed. Suzanne Crawford and Dennis Kelley (Denver, Oxford: ABC–Clio, 2005).

22 Karl Luckert, *Coyoteway* (Tucson: University of Arizona Press, 1979).

23 Washington Matthews, *Blessingway* (1897), p. 109.

Chapter 5

1   See Philip Deloria, *Playing Indian* (New Haven: Yale University Press, 1998); Laurie Ann Whitt, "Cultural Imperialism and the Marketing of Native America," in Devon Mihesuah, ed., *Natives and Academics: Researching and Writing about American Indians* (Lincoln: University of Nebraska Press, 1998); and Ward Churchill, *Fantasies of the Master Race: Literature, Cinema, and the Colonization of American Indians* (San Francisco: City Lights Books, 1998).

2   Cited in Wendy Rose, "The Great Pretenders: Further Reflections on White Shamanism," in *State of Native America: Genocide, Colonization and Resistance* (Cambridge, MA: South End Press, 1992), p. 403.

3   It should also be noted that Native leaders and elders are not necessarily opposed to

teaching spiritual principles to non-Natives. But non-Natives ought not to think they can participate in Native ceremonies without going through the same learning process that a Native person would be required to go through. And such a learning process is neither quick nor convenient. It is a lifelong commitment to community, to an extended family, and to years of relationships with spiritual leaders. Native spiritualities cannot be purchased or acquired within a weekend retreat. Native traditions are inextricably tied to both the landscape and the community itself, and participation in one requires a genuine commitment to the others. See "Declaration of War Against Exploiters of Lakota Spirituality," in Ward Churchill's *Indians R Us?: Culture and Genocide in Native North America* (Toronto: Between the Lines, 1993), pp. 273–7.

4   See Mihesuah 1998.
5   http://www.nau.edu/~hcpo-p/current/hopi_ipr.htm.
6   David Hurst Thomas, *Skull Wars: Kennewick Man, Archaeology, and the Battle for Native American Identity* (Philadelphia: Basic Books, 2000).
7   See Devon Mihesuah, ed., *Repatriation Reader: Who Owns Native American Remains?* (Lincoln: University of Nebraska Press, 2000).
8   See Suzanne Crawford, "(Re)Constructing Bodies: Semiotic Sovereignty and the Debate Over Kennewick Man," in Mihesuah 2000.
9   T.J. Ferguson, Roger Anyon, and Edmund Ladd, "Repatriation at the Pueblo of Zuni: Diverse Solutions to Complex Problems," in Mihesuah 2000.
10 See Thomas Biolsi and Larry Zimmerman, *Indians and Anthropologists: Vine Deloria Jr., and the Critique of Anthropology* (Tucson: University of Arizona Press, 1991).
11 "Digging for Answers: Archaeologists Listen," *Indian Country Today*, July 8, 2003.
12 Crawford 2000.
13 For further information on the AIRF Act of 1978, see Walter Echo Hawk, "Legislation and American Indian Freedom," in *American Indian Religious Traditions: An Encyclopedia*, ed. Suzanne Crawford and Dennis Kelley (Denver, Oxford: ABC–Clio, 2005).
14 For further information on Devil's Tower, Black Mesa, and Mt. Shasta, see *In the Light of Reverence* (Bullfrog Films, 2001).
15 See Edward Lazarus, *Black Hills, White Justice: The Sioux Nation Versus the United States, 1775 to the Present* (Lincoln: University of Nebraska Press, 1999).
16 Pavel, Miller, and Pavel 1993, p. 54.
17 Pavel, Miller, and Pavel 1993, p. 55.
18 Judith Nies, "The Black Mesa Syndrome: Indian Lands, Black Gold," *Orion Magazine*, Summer 1998; http://www.blackmesais.org; see also Emily Benedek, *The Wind Won't Know Me: A History of the Navajo-Hopi Land Dispute* (Norman: University of Oklahoma Press, 1999).
19 Continually updated information on this struggle, as well as ways that individuals can help, can be accessed on the internet at http://www.blackmesais.org/background.htm.
20 Personal communication, Jim Garret, 1998. See also Jim Garrett, "The Cheyenne River Tribal College Tatanka (Bison) Management Program," unpublished Master's thesis, Humboldt State University, Arcata, CA.
21 Jennifer Hemmingsen, "Commission Protects Columbia River Salmon," *Indian Country Today*, July 16, 2002.
22 Cited in Karen Sandrick, "The Wisdom of the Old Ways: Lorelei DeCora's Porcupine Clinic on the Pine Ridge Reservation," *Hospitals and Health Networks*, 71/4 (February 20, 1997), p. 42.

Glossary

Coast Salish terms

Coast Salish A cultural and linguistic group comprised of a variety of diverse nations along the Pacific Northwest Coast, including but not limited to the Nuxalk, Homalco, Klahoose, Sliammon, Sechelt, Squamish, Halq'emeylem, Ostlq'emeylem, Pentlatch, Straits, Klallum, Quileute, Puyallup, Nisqually, Chehalis, Squaxin Island, Skokomish, and Tillamook.

First Salmon ceremony Ceremony honoring the arrival of the first salmon each year, common throughout the Puget Sound and Northwest Coast. Part of a series of other first foods ceremonies, including First Berries, First Elk, and First Roots.

Haik Saib Yo Bouch Chief of the Salmon People.

Indian Shaker Church Church founded by John and Mary Slocum in 1893. A blending of indigenous traditions and Christianity. Not to be confused with the New England movement founded by Mother Ann Lee (the United Society of Believers), also known as the Shakers.

Potlatch Ceremonial tradition common throughout the Northwest coast, in which gifts are distributed and names and rank are conferred.

Raven Trickster figure from Northwest Coast mythology; responsible for liberating the moon and sun and placing them in the sky.

Syó'wən Guardian spirit power; winter ceremonial; winter spirit dances.

Transformer or **Changer** Mythic figure who set the world in order, establishing the proper social, ceremonial, and spiritual relationships between the human people, plant people, and animal people.

Xœ'xœ' Powerful, dangerous, sacred.

Diné terms

Changing Woman Diné Holy Person, the mother of Monster Slayer and Child of the Water. The first to have a *Kinààldá*.

Diné "The people," the Navajo nation.

Hataałii A traditional Diné ceremonialist; a singer who leads chantways.

Hooghan A traditional Diné home, mirroring the cosmos. It is eight-sided, honoring the four directions, and open to the east.

'Iikáah Sand paintings, used in ceremonial chantways. They represent images of the Holy People, and through their creation call the Holy People to be present at a chantway. They act as means through which patients can restore relationships with spiritual beings, and also help to locate a patient within a sacred geography.

Kinàaldá Diné girls' puberty ceremony.

Niłch'i Holy Wind, the animating force in the universe.

Sa'ah Naaghai Bik'eh Hozho Central principle of Diné philosophy, variously translated by scholars as 'long-life happiness," or as the balance of feminine and masculine energies leading to health and fertility.

Yé'ii The Holy People, or Inner Forms of the Diné homeland.

Lakota terms

Haŋbleceyapi "Crying for a Vision." The Lakota vision quest.

Hunkapi Iowanpi "They sing over those over whom the *Hunka* staffs are held," a ceremony of adoption.

Iktomi Spider, the trickster figure in Lakota Creation narratives.

Inipi or *Inikagapi* Sweat lodge ceremony.

Isnati Awicalowan "When she lives alone, they sing over her," a girl's puberty ceremony.

Lakota The Lakota are part of a larger group, the Oceti Sakowin (meaning "the seven places of fire"), and are referred to as the Sioux by Euroamericans. The Oceti Sakowin speak three languages: Lakota, Nakota, and Dakota. The Lakota are comprised of seven bands: Oglala, "they scatter the dust"; Sicanju or Brulé, meaning "burnt thighs"; Hunkpapa, "end of the circle"; Miniconjous, "planters beside the stream"; Sihasapa or Blackfeet; Itazipacola or Sans Arc, meaning "without bows"; and Oohenupa, or "two kettles."

Mitakuye Oyasin "All My Relations," a Lakota blessing and conclusion to prayer; a reminder of one's place in the interconnected universe.

Paha Sapa The Black Hills, or "Heart of all there is."

Tapa Wankeyeyapi "Throwing a ball," a ceremonial game in which a girl throws a ball in the four directions, educating other children about the sacrality and symbolism of the four directions.

Wakan Abstract power animating the universe; sacrality, holiness.

Wakan Tanka Great Mystery; sometimes translated as the sum of all things unknown.

Wanagi Yuhapi "They keep the ghost," a Lakota ceremony of mourning in which a lock of hair is kept, and the individual honored for one year.

White Buffalo Calf Woman Female messiah figure who brought the Lakota the sacred White Buffalo Calf Pipe, seven sacred ceremonies, and buffalo during a time of famine.

Wiwanyang wacipi Lakota Sun Dance.

Wolakota A state of balance, harmony, and good relationship with one's spiritual and human communities.

For further information on these terms see:

Coast Salish

Pamela Amoss, *Coast Salish Spirit Dancing: The Survival of an Ancestral Religion* (Seattle: University of Washington Press, 1978); Crisca Bierwert, *Brushed by Cedar, Living by the River: Salish Figures of Power* (Tucson: University of Arizona Press, 1999).

Diné

Gladys Reichard, *Navajo Religion* (Princeton: Princeton University Press, 1990); James K. McNeley, *Holy Wind in Navajo Philosophy* (Tucson: University of Arizona, 1981).

Lakota

Joseph Epes Brown, *The Gift of the Sacred Pipe: Based on Black Elk's Accounts of the Seven Rites of the Oglala Sioux* (Norman: University of Oklahoma Press, 1982); Mark St. Pierre and Tilda Long Soldier, *Walking in the Sacred Manner* (New York: Simon and Schuster, 1995); James Walker, *Lakota Belief and Ritual* (Lincoln: University of Nebraska Press, 1980).

Pronunciation Guide

Many of the sounds within Native American languages do not translate easily into English phonemes. I have not attempted phonetic renderings of Native terms, as these may be misleading or inaccurate. However, readers may find the following guide helpful.

ʼ	Glottal stop, as in uh-oh!
a	f<u>a</u>ther
č	<u>ch</u>urch
e	y<u>e</u>t
é	<u>eh</u>
ə	sof<u>a</u>, or j<u>u</u>st
i	mach<u>i</u>ne
ł	"tl" or "hl" sound; similar to atlas
ŋ	lu<u>ng</u>
q	<u>c</u>all
u	between r<u>u</u>le and j<u>o</u>ke
š	Engli<u>sh</u>
w	to<u>w</u>er
x	<u>h</u>uge

Suggested Further Reading

THELMA ADAMSON, *Folk-Tales of the Coast Salish* (New York: G.E. Techert and Co, 1934)

LORI ALVORD, *The Scalpel and the Silver Bear: The First Navajo Woman Surgeon Combines Western Medicine and Traditional Healing* (New York: Bantam, 2000)

PAMELA AMOSS, *Coast Salish Spirit Dancing: The Survival of an Ancestral Religion* (Seattle: University of Washington Press, 1978)

PAMELA AMOSS and WILLIAM SEABURG (eds.), *Badger and Coyote Were Neighbors: Melville Jacobs on Northwest Coast Myths and Tales* (Eugene: University of Oregon Press, 2000)

JAMES AXTELL, *The Invasion Within: The Conquest of Cultures in Colonial North America* (Oxford: Oxford University Press, 1986)

H.G. BARNETT, *Indian Shakers: A Messianic Cult of the Pacific Northwest* (Carbondale, IL: Southern Illinois University Press, 1972)

KEITH BASSO, *Wisdom Sits in Places: Landscape and Language Among the Western Apache* (Albuquerque: University of New Mexico Press, 1996)

SHIRLEY BEGAY et al., *Kinààldá: A Navajo Puberty Ceremony* (Phoenix, AZ: Navajo Curriculum Center, 1983)

EMILY BENEDEK, *The Wind Won't Know Me: A History of the Navajo–Hopi Land Dispute* (Norman: University of Oklahoma Press, 1999)

CRISCA BIERWERT, *Brushed By Cedar, Living By the River: Coast Salish Figures of Power* (Tucson: University of Arizona Press, 1999)

FRANZ BOAS, *The Religion of the Kwakiutl* (New York: Columbia University Press, 1930)

MARTIN BROKENLEG, "Ceremony and Ritual, Lakota," in Suzanne Crawford and Dennis Kelley (eds.), *American Indian Religious Traditions: An Encyclopedia* (Oxford: ABC–Clio, 2005)

DAVID BRUGGE, *The Navajo-Hopi Land Dispute: An American Tragedy* (Albuquerque: University of New Mexico Press, 2000)

THOMAS BUCKLEY, "The Shaker Church and the Indian Way in Native Northwestern California," in Lee Irwin (ed.), *Native American Spirituality* (Lincoln: Bison Books, 2000)

RAYMOND BUCKO, *The Lakota Ritual of the Sweat Lodge: History and Contemporary Practice* (Lincoln: University of Nebraska Press, 1998)

JAMES TAYLOR CARSON, *Searching for the Bright Path: The Mississippi Choctaws from Prehistory to Removal* (Lincoln: University of Nebraska Press, 1999)

FAY COHEN, *Treaties on Trial: The Continuing Controversy Over Northwest Indian Fishing Rights* (Seattle: University of Washington Press, 1986)

SUZANNE J. CRAWFORD, "(Re)Constructing Bodies: Semiotic Sovereignty and the Debate Over Kennewick Man," in Devon Mihesuah (ed.), *Repatriation Reader: Who Owns Native American Remains?* (Lincoln: University of Nebraska Press, 2000)

LEONARD CROW DOG, *Crow Dog: Four Generations of Sioux Medicine Men* (New York: Harper Collins, 1996)

MARY CROW DOG, *Lakota Woman* (New York: HarperCollins, 1990)

VINE DELORIA JR., *God is Red: A Native View of Religion* (Golden, CO: Fulcrum, 2003)

RAYMOND DEMALLIE, *The Sixth Grandfather: Black Elk's Teachings to John G. Neihardt* (Lincoln: University of Nebraska Press, 1985)

PHILIP DRUCKER, *Cultures of the North Pacific Coast* (San Francisco: Chandler Publishing Co., 1965)

BARBARA R. DUNCAN, *Living Stories of the Cherokee. With stories told by Davey Arch, Robert Bushyhead, Edna Chekelelee, Marie Junaluska, Kathi Smith Littlejohn, and*

Freeman Owle (Chapel Hill: The University of North Carolina Press, 1998)

CHARLOTTE FRISBIE (ed.), *Southwestern Indian Ritual Drama* (Long Grove, IL: Waveland Press, 1989)

CHARLOTTE JOHNSON FRISBIE, *Kináaldá: A Study of the Navajo Girls' Puberty Ceremony* (Salt Lake City: University of Utah Press, 1993)

JEAN GUY GOULET, *Ways of Knowing: Experience, Knowledge and Power among the Dene Tha* (Lincoln: University of Nebraska, 1998)

TRUDY GRIFFIN-PIERCE, *Earth is My Mother, Sky is My Father: Space, Time, and Astronomy in Navajo Sandpainting* (Albuquerque: University of New Mexico Press, 1995)

JOHN GRIM, "Sun Dance," in Suzanne Crawford and Dennis Kelley (eds.), *American Indian Religious Traditions: An Encyclopedia* (Oxford: ABC–Clio, 2005)

RICHARD GROUNDS, GEORGE TINKER, AND DAVID WILKINS (eds.), *Native Voices: American Indian Identity and Resistance* (Lawrence, KS: University Press of Kansas, 2003)

HOWARD L. HARROD, *Renewing the World: Plains Indian Religion and Morality* (Tucson: University of Arizona Press, 1987)

THOM HESS, *Dictionary of Puget Salish* (Seattle: University of Washington Press, 1976)

MICHAEL HITTMAN, *Wovoka and the Ghost Dance* (Lincoln: University of Nebraska Press, 1998)

FREDERICK HOXIE, *A Final Promise: The Campaign to Assimilate the Indians 1880–1920* (Lincoln: University of Nebraska Press, 2001)

LEE IRWIN, "Freedom, Law, and Prophecy: A Brief History of Native American Religious Resistance," in *Native American Spirituality* (Lincoln: Bison Books, 2000)

TROY JOHNSON, *The Occupation of Alcatraz Island: Indian Self Determination and the Rise of Indian Activism* (Champaign: University of Illinois Press, 1996)

SERGEI KAN, *Symbolic Immortality: The Tlingit Potlatch of the Nineteenth Century* (Washington D.C.: Smithsonian Press, 1989)

CLARA SUE KIDWELL, *Choctaws and Missionaries in Mississippi, 1818–1918* (Norman: University of Oklahoma Press, 1995)

CLARA SUE KIDWELL, HOMER NOLEY, and GEORGE TINKER, *A Native American Theology* (Maryknoll: Orbis Books, 2001)

ANDREW KNAUT, *The Pueblo Revolt of 1680: Conquest and Resistance in Seventeenth Century New Mexico* (Norman: University of Oklahoma Press, 1997)

LUKE LASSITER, CLYDE ELLIS, and RALPH KOTAY, *The Jesus Road: Kiowas, Christianity, and Indian Hymns* (Lincoln: University of Nebraska, 2002)

JERROLD LEVY, *In the Beginning: The Navajo Genesis* (Berkeley: University of California Press, 1998)

ELIZABETH L. LEWTON and VICTORIA BYDONE, "Identity and Healing in Three Navajo Religious Traditions: Sa'ah Naaghai Bik'eh Hozho," *Medical Anthropology Quarterly* 14/4 (2000): pp. 476–97

KARL LUCKERT, *Coyoteway* (Tucson: University of Arizona Press, 1979)

THOMAS E. MAILS, *Sundancing at Rosebud and Pine Ridge* (Sioux Falls: Center for Western Studies, Augustana College, 1978)

JOEL MARTIN, *The Land Looks After Us: A History of Native American Religion* (Oxford: Oxford University Press, 2001)

JOEL W. MARTIN, *Sacred Revolt: The Muskogees' Struggle for a New World* (East Sussex: Beacon Press, 1991)

MICHAEL MCNALLY, *Ojibwe Singers: Hymns, Grief and a Native Culture in Motion* (Oxford: Oxford University Press, 2000)

JAMES K. MCNELEY, *Holy Wind in Navajo Philosophy* (Tucson: University of Arizona Press, 1981)

DEVON MIHESUAH, *Repatriation Reader: Who Owns Native American Remains?* (Lincoln: University of Nebraska Press, 2000)

JAY MILLER, *Shamanic Odyssey: The Lushootseed Salish Journey to the Land of the Dead* (Menlo Park: Ballena Press, 1989)

JAY MILLER, *Lushootseed Culture and Shamanic Odyssey: An Anchored Radiance* (Lincoln: University of Nebraska Press, 1999)

JAMES MOONEY, *The Ghost Dance Religion and Wounded Knee* (Mineola, NY: Dover, 1991)

JOHN G. NEIHARDT, *Black Elk Speaks* (Lincoln: Bison Books, 2003)

RICHARD K. NELSON, *Make Prayers to the Raven: A Koyukon View of the Northern Forest* (Chicago: University of Chicago, 1986)

ALFONSO ORTIZ, *Tewa World: Space, Time and Becoming in a Pueblo Society* (Chicago: University of Chicago, 1972)

PAMELA OWENS, "Trail of Tears," in *American Indian Religious Traditions: An Encyclopedia* (Oxford: ABC–Clio, 2005)

NANCY PAREZO, *Navajo Sandpainting: From Ceremonial Act to Commercial Art* (Albuquerque: University of New Mexico Press, 1991, reprint edition)

THOMAS C. PARKHILL, *Weaving Ourselves Into the Land: Charles Godfrey Leland, "Indians," and the Study of Native American Religions* (Albany, NY: State University Press of New York, 1997)

D. MICHAEL PAVEL, GERALD B. MILLER, and MARY J. PAVEL, "Too Long Too Silent: The Threat to Cedar and the Sacred Ways of the Skokomish," *American Indian Culture and Research Journal* 17/3 (1993), pp. 53–80

THEDA PERDUE, *Nations Remembered: An Oral History of the Cherokees, Chickasaws, Choctaws, Creeks, and Seminoles in Oklahoma, 1865–1907* (Norman: University of Oklahoma Press, 1993)

MARLA POWERS, *Oglala Women: Myth, Ritual and Reality* (Chicago: University of Chicago Press, 1983)

WILLIAM K. POWERS, *Oglala Religion* (Lincoln: University of Nebraska Press, 1977)

GLADYS REICHARD, *Navajo Religion* (Princeton: Princeton University Press, 1990)

WENDY ROSE, "The Great Pretenders: Further Reflections on White Shamanism," in *State of Native America: Genocide, Colonization and Resistance* (Cambridge, MA: South End Press, 1992)

ROBERT RUBY and JOHN BROWN, *John Slocum and the Indian Shaker Church* (Norman: University of Oklahoma Press, 1996)

MAUREEN TRUDELLE SCHWARZ, *Molded in the Image of Changing Woman: Navajo Views on the Human Body and Personhood* (Tucson: University of Arizona Press, 1997)

MARK ST. PIERRE, *Madonna Swan: A Lakota Woman's Story* (Norman: University of Oklahoma Press, 1994)

MARK ST. PIERRE and TILDA LONG SOLDIER, *Walking in the Sacred Manner* (New York: Simon and Schuster, 1995)

WAYNE SUTTLES, *Coast Salish Essays* (Seattle: University of Washington Press, 1987)

WAYNE SUTTLES (ed.), *Handbook of North American Indians: Northwest Coast* (Washington D.C.: Smithsonian Press, 1990)

JOHN R. SWANTON, *Creek Religion and Medicine* (Lincoln: University of Nebraska Press, 2000, reprint edition)

DAVID HURST THOMAS, *Skull Wars: Kennewick Man, Archaeology, and the Battle for Native American Identity* (Philadelphia: Basic Books, 2000)

GEORGE TINKER, *Missionary Conquest: The Gospel and Native American Cultural Genocide* (Minneapolis: Fortress, 2003, reprint edition)

JAMES TREAT, *Native and Christian: Indigenous Voices on Religious Identity in the United States and Canada* (New York: Routledge, 1995)

ROBERT A. TRENNERT, *White Man's Medicine: Government Doctors and the Navajo, 1863–1955* (Albuquerque: University of New Mexico, 1998)

JAMES WALKER, RAYMOND J. DEMALLIE, and ELAINE A. JAHNER (eds.), *Lakota Belief and Ritual* (Lincoln: University of Nebraska Press, 1980)

JAMES WALKER, *Lakota Myth* (Lincoln: University of Nebraska Press, 1983)

JACE WEAVER, *Native American Religious Identity: Unforgotten Gods* (Maryknoll: Orbis, 1998)

RICHARD WHITE, *The Middle Ground: Indians, Empires and Republics in the Great Lakes Region, 1650–1815* (Cambridge: Cambridge University Press, 1991)

LAURIE ANN WHITT, "Cultural Imperialism and the Marketing of Native America," in Devon Mihesuah (ed.), *Natives and Academics: Researching and Writing About American Indians* (Lincoln: University of Nebraska Press, 1998)

THOMAS YELLOWTAIL, *Yellowtail: Crow Medicine Man and Sun Dance Chief* (Lincoln: University of Oklahoma Press, 1991)

PAUL ZOBROD, *Diné Bahane': The Navajo Creation Story* (Albuquerque: University of New Mexico, 1988)

FILMS

Heart of the People (Gryphon Productions, 1996)

In the Light of Reverence (Bullfrog Films, 2001)

Incident at Oglala (Artisan Films, 1994)

Kinààldá: Navajo Rite of Passage (Women Make Movies, 2002)

Rendering of Wealth (1999)

Return of the River (Gryphon Productions, 2000)

Seasons of a Navajo (Peace River Films and PBS Home Video, 1985, re-released 2000)

The Peyote Road: Ancient Religion in Contemporary Crisis (Kafaru Productions, 1995)

Index